Knock

19/4/2008

NEWMAN'S APPROACH
TO KNOWLEDGE

NEWMAN'S APPROACH TO KNOWLEDGE

Laurence Richardson

GRACEWING

First published in 2007

Gracewing
2 Southern Avenue
Leominster
Herefordshire HR6 0QF

UK ISBN 0 85244 094 4
978 0 85244 094 0

Typeset by Action Publishing Technology Ltd,
Gloucester GL1 5SR

CONTENTS

FOREWORD

by John F. Crosby

Dr Richardson is right; Newman's work is very important indeed for philosophers, far more important than they commonly recognize. Dr Richardson makes a contribution to the study of Newman by writing a book that centres around the philosophical significance of his work. I myself teach and write as a philosopher, and Newman's work has been inestimably important for me. In recent years I have been drawn into the orbit of what is called Christian personalism and I have tried to contribute something towards an understanding of persons and the personal. Thinkers such as Max Scheler, Dietrich von Hildebrand, and Karol Wojtyla have been major sources of my thinking on personalism; but Newman has also been a major source, and just as important in his own way as any of the others. Take for instance Newman's idea of the 'illative sense' as developed in *The Grammar of Assent*; Newman explores in a most original way how it is that the individual person thinks and reasons and forms beliefs, and in fact *puts his individual personality into his thinking and reasoning*. It is a contribution towards a more personalist epistemology. Edward Sillem, one of Dr Richardson's predecessors in the study of Newman's philosophy, rightly said: Newman 'stands at the threshold of the new age as a Christian Socrates, the pioneer of a new philosophy of the Individual Person and Personal Life'.

Dr Richardson is exactly right, I think, in detecting a particular affinity of Newman with phenomenological philosophy. I have always thought of Newman as a kind of proto-phenomenologist. For Newman is always trying to make us *realize* the truth; too many people profess truth notionally without *realizing* it, and he wants to awaken in them the *experience* of what they profess. In the language of Husserl we could say that too many people remain at the level of *empty meaning-intentions* and fail to achieve any *intuitive fulfillment* of these intentions.

By calling out to philosophers, '*zurück zu den Sachen selbst!*' or 'back to the things themselves!' Husserl wanted to turn philosophers back to the sources of experience or intuition. This is in a way the genius of phenomenology – to recover the experience of being and truth and to learn to do philosophy with rigorous and disciplined attention to the way being shows itself in our experience. And this is deeply akin to Newman's attempt to convert notional assent into real assent. It is true that Newman is not always dealing with specifically philosophical assents, as when he tries in his sermons to lead his listeners to a greater realization of revealed truth. And yet even here there is this point of kinship between Newman and phenomenology: they both aim at recovering the sources of experience.

This phenomenological bent of Newman's mind shows itself in a particular way in the philosophy of religion. In one place he complains that the attributes ascribed by theology to God 'are drawn out as if on paper, as we might map a country we had never seen'. Then he asks, 'Can I attain to any more vivid assent to the Being of a God, than that which is given merely to notions of the intellect? Can I rise to what I have called an imaginative apprehension of it? Can I believe as if I saw?' He proceeds to give his famous account of how the experience of moral obligation can be read so that we can indeed come to believe as if we saw. Newman was one of the first thinkers to explore a more experiential approach to God, not of course as a substitute for theology but as a complement to it. With this he opened the door to the philosophy of religion as distinct from natural theology. Newman would have rejoiced to read works like Rudolf Otto's *The Idea of the Holy* (1917) and Max Scheler's *On the Eternal in Man* (1921); he would have seen in these works a philosophical reflection on exactly the experiential element in religion that he was trying to articulate more than half a century earlier. Scheler, by the way, was well aware of Newman as his predecessor. He read Newman, learned much from him, and often referred to him. Scheler entirely understood the originality of Newman in the philosophy of religion.

Dr Richardson understands this as well. This is why he has written a book that presents and analyses Newman the philosopher, examining both the rootedness of Newman in the tradition of Christian philosophy and at the same time appreciating the novelty and modernity of Newman. He has given us another competent guide for the study of Newman as philosopher.

John F. Crosby

Dr John F. Crosby is Professor of Philosophy at the Franciscan University of Steubenville, Ohio. He studied under Dietrich von Hildebrand and has published some fifteen articles on the thought of Newman. He is also the author of *Selfhood of the Human Person* (1996) and *Personalist Papers* (2004).

ABBREVIATIONS AND REFERENCES

The usual abbreviations for Newman's works are used in the text. For instance, *An Essay in Aid of a Grammar of Assent* is referred to as the *Grammar of Assent* or simply the *Grammar*, and *Apologia pro Vita Sua* as *Apologia*.

The endnotes to each chapter employ the customary abbreviations listed below. They are those proposed by Joseph Rickaby in his *Index to the Works of John Henry Cardinal Newman* (London, 1914). They also include those suggested by Charles Stephen Dessain in *The Letters and Diaries of John Henry Newman*. I have taken the liberty to simplify some by omitting unnecessary punctuation.

Unless otherwise stated all references to the works of Newman are those of the uniform edition of 1868–1881 (thirty-six volumes), published by Longmans, Green and Company of London. There is a reprint of this edition by Christian Classics Incorporated, Westminster, Maryland, USA, 1973.

Page references given of the *Grammar of Assent* are to the first fully annotated critical edition published in 1985. It was edited, with introduction and notes, by Ian Ker. This edition has the advantage of possibly being more readily available than any of the earlier editions. In parenthesis I also give the corresponding reference to the eighth and last edition published during Newman's lifetime. This appeared in 1889 and forms part of the uniform edition.

The notes at the end of each chapter include sufficient bibliographical information to identify each source. Full details will be found in the Bibliography.

Apo: *Apologia pro Vita Sua*

AW: *John Henry Newman: Autobiographical Writings*

Dev: *An Essay on the Development of Christian Doctrine*

Diff I, II: *Certain Difficulties Felt by Anglicans in Catholic Teaching*, 2 vols

Ess I, II: *Essays Critical and Historical*, 2 vols

GA: *An Essay in Aid of a Grammar of Assent*

Gregorianum: 'The Newman-Perrone Paper on Development (*De Catholici dogmatis evolutione*)', *Gregorianum*, vol. 16 (1935)

HS I, II, III: *Historical Sketches*, 3 vols

Idea: *The Idea of a University Defined and Illustrated*

LD I–XXXI: *The Letters and Diaries of John Henry Newman*, 31 vols

Mir I, II: *Two Essays on Biblical and on Ecclesiastical Miracles*, 2 vols

Mix: *Discourses Addressed to Mixed Congregations*

Moz I, II: *Letters and Correspondence of John Henry Newman During His Life in the English Church*, 2 vols

OA: Birmingham Oratory Archives

OS: *Sermons Preached on Various Occasions*

Phil N II: *The Philosophical Notebook of John Henry Newman*

Prepos: *Present Position of Catholics in England*

PS I–VIII: *Parochial and Plain Sermons*, 8 vols

SD: *Sermons Bearing on Subjects of the Day*

SE: *Stray Essays on Controversial Points*

TP I: *The Theological Papers of John Henry Newman on Faith and Certainty*

TP II: *Theological Papers of John Henry Newman on Biblical Inspiration and on Infallibility*

US: *Fifteen Sermons Preached Before the University of Oxford*

INTRODUCTION

It was while immersed in research for my doctoral thesis on the ecclesiology of John Henry Newman that I came to realize his love for philosophy. And at the same time the importance he gave to it as the basis on which to build a truly coherent theology. The present short volume is the result of my subsequent research on Newman the philosopher. The great value he gave to philosophy can easily be appreciated by reading his discourse, *Knowledge Its Own End*, in his *Idea of a University*. He argues for the benefit of a faculty of Philosophy in a university, not only as something good in itself, but also as providing a vital link with, and service to, all the other sciences. He affirms: 'Not to know the relative disposition of things is the state of slaves or children; to have mapped out the Universe is the boast, or at least the ambition, of Philosophy.'[1]

For many years Newman cherished the ambition of writing a treatise on philosophy.[2] In 1859 he began to compile a notebook on philosophical topics in preparation for this venture. He even gave it the tentative title of *Discursive Enquiries on Metaphysical Subjects*. Unfortunately this enterprise never came to fruition. Nevertheless, much of his mature philosophical thought did come to light in 1870 with the publication of his *Grammar of Assent*. Although the primordial aim of this work was theological its argument rests on a firm philosophical foundation. This is the context in which we find the primary source for his philosophy.

The methodology I have used in this appraisal of Newman's approach to philosophy is to consider his thought in the light of a more familiar philosophical framework. This facilitates the analysis of his philosophy by making it possible to draw comparisons, or to highlight differences, with respect to the chosen frame of reference. At the same time I hope that this will make it easier to appreciate Newman's insights when seen in the context of a more familiar reference frame. For this role I have chosen the philosophy of St Thomas Aquinas. At first sight, to those already familiar with Newman's way of thinking, such a method might seem questionable. He is manifestly individualistic in his approach. He does not follow any particular philosophical trend, including that of the scholastics. As pointed out by Edmond D. Benard and Sylvester P. Juergens, such observations are valid.[3] However, my method does not imply any systematic, concept by concept, comparison between his thought and that of Aquinas. Being such an independent thinker any endeavour of this kind would be prone to distorting his view. In the past, as noted by Ian Ker and Juergens, such attempts to do this have not been helpful to the cause of Newman as philosopher.[4] It is certainly not my intention to force his thought into some kind of preconceived mould, thomistic or otherwise.

The prejudices of unfriendly critics of his philosophy can often form a barrier preventing them from entering fully into Newman's thought. This can result in them being quick to dismiss, or condemn, what they do not fully understand. Even during his lifetime he was obliged to defend his position against those who attacked him for not holding the then current scholastic vision of epistemology.[5]

Alternatively, friendly commentators sometimes fall into the trap of being so hasty to see their own cherished ideas reflected in his thought that they overlook the danger of misinterpretation. This was the case of those authors who attempted to associate his views with modernism at the beginning of the twentieth century.[6] As Etienne Gilson affirms, his philosophy must be approached with a truly open mind, free from any pre-determined prejudices.[7] It is essential to be prepared for the originality and depth found in his thought. Failure to do this may lead to misunderstanding. I think Stanley L. Jaki expressed it very well when he remarked that the *Grammar*, 'looked at superficially, is an amalgam of empiricism, phenomenology and personalism'.[8]

In the thought both of Aquinas and Newman we find the affirmation that inherent in man's nature is his ability to know reality. In his *Grammar* Newman states: 'What is once true is always true; and the human mind is made for truth, and so rests in truth, as it cannot rest in falsehood.'[9] Such an approach to realism, shared in common with Aquinas, serves as a warrant for my methodology. This fundamental tenet of a realist philosophy highlights a basic similarity between the thought of Newman and that of my frame of reference. Philosophy is the quest for truth, to know reality and to seek scientific explanations as to its ultimate causes. As a consequence it is feasible that two independent philosophers may present the same truth for our consideration, not only expressing it using their own particular terminology, but also on the grounds of differing evidence and rational arguments. In this sense I think that there is substantial agreement in many of the conclusions reached by both Aquinas and Newman. Benard and Jaki are of the same opinion.[10] It is this general agreement with respect to the conclusions of Aquinas and Newman that justifies my methodology. At the same time there can be a clear acknowledgement of the differences in their respective approaches to philosophy. Even Newman himself would seem to agree on this point. In a letter following a declaration by Pope Leo XIII in favour of the philosophy of Aquinas, he wrote: 'I have no suspicion, and do not anticipate, that I shall be found in substance to disagree with St. Thomas.'[11]

I take for granted that the reader is familiar with the fundamental concepts of the philosophy of Aquinas. Consequently I consider it superfluous to make many references to his works. Similarly I avoid any pedantic use of thomistic terminology. However, wherever it is essential in terms of clarity, I do mention terms or concepts familiar to the student of Aquinas.

The *Grammar* was published on 15 March 1870 when Newman was in his seventieth year, and sold out during the same day.[12] Unlike many of his other writings this book was not just an occasional essay, the consequence of some historical event. Of all his works it is arguably the closest we have to being a systematic treatise. He himself referred to it as the 'hardest' and 'last' of the 'five constructive books' that he had written.[13] It saw the light of day after a great deal of intellectual reflection on the subject over a period of many years.[14] In a letter of December 1868, referring to the progress he was making, he says that it was 'like tunnelling through a mountain – I have begun it, and it is almost too much for my strength ... Perhaps the tunnel will break in, when I get fairly into my work'.[15] Shortly after its publication, in another letter, he remarks: 'However, any how I have got a great burden off my mind – for twenty or thirty years I have felt it a sort of duty to write upon it.'[16] It was an immediate success and continued to be so. In 1883 he writes: 'The book has succeeded in twelve years far more than I expected. It has reached five full editions.'[17] The last edition published during his lifetime was the eighth. He was happy with his work.[18] As Ker notices, this can be seem from the fact that this last edition of 1889 appeared without any serious alterations to the original, but rather just stylistic in nature.[19] Newman stipulated that: 'If any new edition is called for after my death, it should be printed according to the text of the last edition published in my life time.'[20] Without a shadow of a doubt this work can be considered as the definitive intellectual fruit of his philosophical thought. Gilson affirmed that: 'The *Grammar of Assent* has preserved intact its power of suggestion, its actuality and its fecundity as a method of investigation whose potentialities are far from being exhausted.'[21]

The main purpose for writing his *Grammar* was to describe the process by which the human mind is able to make an act of religious faith. Its aim was to justify, on the strongest of philosophical and theological grounds, that this was an act of the intellect.[22] That is to say, he uses his theory of knowledge explained in the *Grammar* to show that the act of religious faith is perfectly consistent with our rational nature. As an Anglican pastor Newman had agonized for years before becoming a Roman Catholic at the age of forty-three. His journey of faith had been slow, yet always with the greatest intellectual rigour and honesty. Later in life as a consequence of his pastoral work he was greatly struck by the fact that that same religious faith was just as firmly held, with an assent of the intellect, whether by an educated person or by someone who lacked any formal learning. In the *Grammar* he argues that faith is neither the result of some blind impulse, nor just the consequence of religious sentiment or feeling. Religious faith is an act of the intellect appropriate to the dignity of our rational nature. His endeavour was to counter the errors in this respect inherent in the liberalism and rationalism of the day. The liberal faction was inclined to see religious faith either as purely a matter of personal opinion, or that it was only for the simpleminded and emotionally weak. On the other hand, the rationalist tendency was to accept the individual contents of divine revelation only after they could be proved logically.

In the *Grammar* Newman considers religious faith as a human act and does not deal with the strictly supernatural factors involved. That is to say, he discusses the various operations of the intellect that lead to the possible judgement of credibility. He also presents evidence and argues for the reasonableness of believing in Christianity. Given its main objective the *Grammar*, strictly speaking, belongs in the domain of philosophy of religion. However, he clearly recognized the importance of grounding his theology on a solid philosophical foundation. Referring to the *Grammar* on one occasion he said: 'It is half theological, half philosophical.'[23] As Frederick Copleston comments, this philosophical basis is clearly discernible, and it is within this context we find his gnoseology.[24] With a little care, as Charles Stephen Dessain advises, it is relatively easy to distinguish the philosophical elements from the theological; his theory of knowledge from the act of religious faith.[25] The *Grammar* is the primary source of Newman's approach to knowledge. In a note he included in the edition of 1880 he states: 'A main reason for my writing this Essay on Assent, to which I am adding these last words, was, as far as I could, to describe the *organum investigandi* which I thought the true one.'[26]

Any suggestion that Newman tailored his philosophy in the *Grammar* to suit his theological purpose is not sustainable. The most elementary acquaintance with his character and writings clearly manifests his moral integrity and love for the truth. He wrote of himself: 'I have never sinned against the light.'[27] His integrity can be seen, for example, by the way he reacted to a public accusation of intellectual dishonesty by the chaplain of Queen Victoria, Charles Kingsley (1819–1875). This author had become popular with his historical novel, *Westward Ho!*, and his book for children, *The Water-Babies*. In 1864 Kingsley wrote in an article for a magazine, 'Father Newman informs us that the truth for its own sake need not be, and on the whole ought not to be, a virtue of the Roman clergy.'[28] Newman's immediate answer to this blatant taunt was to write a book, *Apologia pro Vita Sua*, which he completed in just ten weeks. This autobiography presents a masterly account of his life and journey of faith. It achieved universal acclaim for its candour and depth, and established his intellectual honesty beyond the slightest doubt. Kingsley declined to write a reply.

Just such integrity is found both in Aquinas and Newman. Their theological writings exhibit the harmony, while acknowledging the differences, between the truths derived from reason and those given to us through divine revelation. They both show that reason and faith are complementary ways of knowing the one reality of God and his created universe. Consequently, as James Collins notes, the philosophical content of their writings is able to stand on its own merits independent of the various theological contexts or objectives.[29]

Although the main argument of the *Grammar* had been maturing in Newman's mind over a period of years it did have its historical occasion. Or perhaps it might be more appropriate to use the word catalyst. William Froude belonged to the circle of friends who had supported him during his time at Oxford University. However, although he was well disposed, he had not become a Roman Catholic like so many of his other friends. He was convinced that the faith of many Roman Catholics was the result of religious sentiment and lacked any genuine intellectual justification.[30] Over a period of years Newman had tried to explain to his friend that this was not the case, 'that a given individual, high or low, has as much right (has as real rational grounds) to be certain, as a learned theologian who knows the scientific evidence'.[31] He was adamant that religious faith was the consequence of a free and personal intellectual assent, appropriate to the dignity of human nature.

In this sense the *Grammar* was his answer to Froude's difficulty. Newman establishes the philosophical grounds upon which he considers the supernatural act of religious faith to be based. Along with Edward Sillem I think that a certain parallel can be drawn between his *Apologia* and the *Grammar*.[32] The former is an autobiographical account of how he came to accept the Catholic faith in practice. The latter explains the philosophical and theological grounds of the intellectual process that led him to make this radical change in his life.

In my presentation of Newman's philosophy I invariably try to let him speak for himself. I agree with Benard who commented that: 'Newman can speak for himself much better than anyone else can speak for him.'[33] Accordingly, I liberally quote from his writings. Likewise, I present the evidence that he himself brings to bear in each discussion, together with the rational arguments that he employs to warrant his conclusions. I feel that this is the best way to do justice to his thought. I think Newman himself would approve of such an approach. In his *Grammar* he affirms that in the fields of metaphysics and ethics:

Egotism is true modesty ... each of us can speak only for himself, and for himself he has a right to speak. His own experiences are enough for himself, but he cannot speak for others: he cannot lay down the law; he can only bring his own experiences to the common stock of psychological facts.[34]

In his published works he is usually very temperate in his use of technical language. However, in the *Grammar* he makes use of some specific terminology. On many occasions he indicates such words by giving them an initial capital letter. For the sake of clarity I adopt this same procedure in my text.

There are several secondary sources for his philosophy. In the main they were written prior to the publication of his *Grammar* in 1870. By and large they do not add a great deal of new material, in terms of philosophy, that did not find its way into the primary source in some form or other. Their value lies chiefly in

terms of confirming or completing his thought. They also serve
to trace its homogeneous development and to show its general
consistency over the years.

Among the more important of these secondary sources are his
University Sermons. These were preached between 1826 and
1843 during the period that he was the Anglican vicar of St
Mary's church, Oxford. They deal with some of the topics, and
pose some of the questions, which later are discussed and
answered in his *Grammar*.[35]

His notes on various philosophical topics that he began to
compile in January 1859, which includes material dated as late
as 1888, are of similar value. They were subsequently published
under the title *The Philosophical Notebook of John Henry
Newman*. I agree with A. J. Boekraad, the co-editor with Sillem,
of the *Notebook* that it must not be considered as representing
Newman's definitive thought.[36] They are notes on philosophical
subjects that occurred to him from time to time, some occa-
sioned by his reading. He expresses himself freely with no
particular attempt to be precise or to give any logical cogency to
his ideas. In an entry of 1888 he referred to these notes in the
following manner: 'What I write, I do not state dogmatically, but
categorically that is, in investigation, nor have I confidence
enough in what I have advanced to warrant publication.'[37] To do
justice to Newman the provisional and tentative nature of this
Notebook should be respected. Consequently we should neither
be over-critical about their content, nor expect a completeness
that was never intended. However, they are particularly useful in
tracing the history of some of the concepts that later find their
definitive expression in the *Grammar*.

*The Theological Papers of John Henry Newman on Faith and
Certainty* is the title given to another collection of his notes that
have since been published. These comprise of a series of
preparatory drafts for possible publication written during the
years 1846 to 1890. As their title suggests they relate mainly to
topics concerning faith and reason. They are of interest since
they contain several texts which show the development of some
of his ideas that eventually became part of his *Grammar*. In
general, in his notes and papers that were not intended for publi-

cation, he makes some use of underlining. This will be indicated with italics in the quotations taken from these notes in my text.

When Newman was the rector of the newly founded Catholic University in Dublin he gave a series of lectures on the nature of university education. These were published in 1852 under the title, *The Idea of a University, Defined and Illustrated*. They contain many interesting aspects of his gnoseology as applied to education.

His *Development of Christian Doctrine* and *Apologia pro Vita Sua* represent minor sources. Their value lies in providing evidence as to the continuity and general consistency of his philosophical thought.

The following pages present an overall picture of Newman's philosophy with a particular focus on his theory of knowledge. The opening chapter is a survey of his philosophical education and the major influences that shaped his thought. The second chapter presents the basic concepts that form the foundation of his philosophy. The subsequent four chapters deal with his approach to the theory of knowledge, and consider his views of Apprehension, Assent, Inference and the Illative Sense. The Illative Sense constitutes one of his more original contributions to gnoseology. The last chapter begins with a presentation of some of the major insights that I consider as comprising his contribution to the progress of contemporary philosophy. I then show that it is possible to classify Newman as a latent forerunner of the phenomenological movement. Some speculation is included as to whether he might also be listed among the pioneers of the realist movement that became known as Oxford philosophy. Finally, I predict a bright future for his thought and his world wide recognition as a philosopher.

It is now over two hundred years since the birth of John Henry Newman. He has long been acknowledged as an outstanding nineteenth-century theologian and literary genius. On the other hand, his universal recognition as a philosopher is long overdue. It is my hope that this little tome will contribute towards such an acknowledgement, and to his rightful inclusion within the history of contemporary philosophy.

The final words of the Newman scholar Johannes Artz in an

essay on Newman's philosophy provide an appropriate conclusion to this introduction, and an apt summary of my objective in writing this book:

> Let us consider it as one of our significant tasks to give Newman his place in the history of philosophy. He was not indeed a systematic professional philosopher, but he did give us important philosophical stimuli and also the rudiments of a system. Let us fulfill our task not by a blind enthusiastic adulation, but critically. What he has begun with such suggestive originality must be brought to full mature fruition.[38]

Notes

1. *Idea*, p. 113.
2. Cf. *AW*, p. 269; *TP* I, p. xii; Ward, vol. I, pp. 423–8; Sillem, pp. 241–8.
3. Cf. Benard, p. 70; Juergens, *Newman on the Psychology of Faith in the Individual*, p. 18.
4. Cf. Ker, 'Introduction', in *GA* (1985), p. lv; Juergens, 'What is Newman's Deepest Message?'
5. Cf. *TP* I, pp. 140–57.
6. Cf. Sillem, pp. 17–18; Ker gives an interesting account of the criticism provoked by the *Grammar* in his 'Introduction', in *GA* (1985), pp. l–lvii.
7. Cf. Gilson, 'Introduction', in *GA* (1955), p. 10; Bacchus, *How to Read the Grammar of Assent*, p. 106; Collins, pp. 27–8.
8. Jaki, *Newman's Challenge*, p. 230.
9. *GA*, p. 145 (221).
10. Cf. Benard, p. 194; Jaki, *Newman's Challenge*, p. 215.
11. Letter to Fr Whitty cited by Tristam, 'Introduction', in Flanagan, p. ix; cf. Davis, p. 159.
12. Cf. *LD* XXV, p. 54.
13. *LD* XXIV, p. 391; cf. *LD* XXV, pp. 11, 35; *LD* XXXV, pp. 34, 51; Ward, vol. II, pp. 262, 266.
14. Cf. *LD* XXV, p. 199; Sillem, p. 167; Dessain, *John Henry Newman*, p. 148; Ward, vol. II, pp. 261–2.
15. *LD* XXIV, p. 184; cf. *LD* XXV, p. 35.

16. Letter to Coleridge, 13 March 1870, quoted in Ward, vol. II, p. 268; cf. *LD* XIV, p. 205; *LD* XIX, p. 500; *LD* XXIV, pp. 74, 389; *LD* XXV, pp. 36, 155; *AW*, pp. 271–3.
17. *LD* XXX, p. 191; cf. *TP* I, p. 140.
18. Cf. *LD* XXV, pp. 160, 279.
19. Cf. Ker, 'Introduction', in *GA* (1985). p. 1.
20. *LD* XXXI, p. 65.
21. Gilson, 'Introduction', in *GA* (1955), pp. 20–1; cf. ibid., p. 9.
22. Cf. Ker's scholarly history of the development of the *Grammar* in Newman's thought in his 'Introduction', in *GA* (1985), pp. xxxii–l.
23. *LD* XXIV, p. 184
24. Cf. Copleston, vol. VIII, p. 516 footnote 2.
25. Dessain, *Cardinal Newman on the Theory and Practice of Knowledge*, p. 9.
26. *GA*, p. 321 (499).
27. *Moz* I, pp. 365–6.
28. Kingsley, article in *MacMillan's Magazine*, January 1864.
29. Cf. Collins, p. 18.
30. Cf. Dessain, *John Henry Newman*, pp. 148, 151, 152; Sillem, pp. 76, 244–6.
31. *LD* XIX, p. 294.
32. Cf. Sillem, pp. 92–3.
33. Benard, p. 200.
34. *GA*, p. 248 (384).
35. Cf. *LD* XXV, p. 35.
36. Cf. Boekraad, 'Preface', in *Phil N* II, p. 5.
37. *Phil N* II, p. 6.
38. Artz, 'Newman as Philosopher', p. 287.

CHAPTER 1

THE PHILOSOPHER

John Henry Cardinal Newman (1801–1890) has long been universally recognized as one of the most outstanding theologians and literary geniuses of the nineteenth century. Pope John Paul II in his Encyclical, *Fides et ratio*, on the relationship between faith and reason, gave him first place among his nine examples of outstanding contemporary, 'Christian theologians who also distinguished themselves as great philosophers'.[1] Alas, his endeavours in the field of philosophy have been somewhat overlooked, both among academics and especially in the world at large. Edward Sillem, a Newman scholar, laments: 'In the philosophical world as a whole, Newman's right to be considered a philosopher has scarcely been considered till comparatively recently, ... Few historians of philosophy make any mention of him when they come to write about the nineteenth century.'[2] However, judging by the interest shown in his thought during the past few decades, this situation is gradually changing and his reputation as a significant nineteenth-century philosopher is growing. The number of contemporary authors who have considered his philosophical views worthy of serious attention is increasing. Among these we might mention Jean Guitton, Etienne Gilson, A. J. Boekraad, Bernard Lonergan, Jan Hendrik Walgrave, James Collins, Frederick Copleston, Edward Sillem, Johannes Artz, Ian Ker and Stanley L. Jaki.

Gilson, the renowned philosopher, in his introduction to a 1955 edition of Newman's *Grammar of Assent* affirmed that: 'It is desirable to emphasize the originality of an undertaking whose importance is even more evident in our times than it was in 1870.'[3] Lonergan, philosopher and theologian, published his well known work, *Insight*, in 1957. He acknowledged the influence of Newman on his own thinking.[4] Walgrave, writing in 1957, states that he was a 'veritable philosopher and a great figure in philosophy'.[5] In 1961 Collins wrote: 'A fresh assessment of Newman's significance for philosophy is also being made by many scholars, who are now sufficiently removed from the controversy over Modernism to permit them to take a calmer and more accurate look.'[6] Copleston, in volume eight of his authoritative *History of Philosophy*, first published in 1966, included a substantial appendix on the thought of Newman.[7] In this same volume it is interesting to note those nineteenth-century philosophers who, in the judgement of Copleston, merited about the same number of pages. In this category we find Jeremy Bentham (1748–1832), the British exponent of utilitarianism, William James (1842–1910), the American pragmatist and Bernard Bosanquet (1848–1923), the British idealist. And, if we include those to whom he dedicated just a few pages more, then we have Josiah Royce (1855–1916), the American idealist and George Edward Moore (1873–1958), the British common sense realist. Ker acknowledges that Sillem has given us 'the fullest and most detailed study of Newman's philosophy'.[8] This scholar, in his introductory volume to *The Philosophical Notebook of John Henry Newman*, written in 1969, even went so far as to affirm that if Newman had completed his planned treatise on philosophy then, he 'might even now be recognised as a modern St Augustine in Christian philosophical circles'.[9] In 1976 Artz, after advocating Newman's recognition as a philosopher, wrote that: 'He was not indeed a systematic professional philosopher, but he did give us important philosophical stimuli and also the rudiments of a system.'[10]

In a certain sense it is understandable that his recognition as a notable philosopher has been slow in dawning. As just mentioned in my quotation from Artz, he was not a professional philosopher. Furthermore, he never achieved his ambition of publishing a treatise on the subject. In this respect Sillem says that:

He had no chance of showing himself as such to the world during his life, and he had no special interest in being known as a philosopher in his lifetime. ... To those who knew Newman ... it is clear that by nature he was indeed a strikingly original philosopher who might have achieved renown had he so aspired.[11]

Another reason, as observed by Copleston, for him being overlooked in history is the difficulty of placing his thought within any of the other philosophical currents of the nineteenth century. He then adds, referring to his own survey of Newman's philosophy, that to omit him 'because of the difficulty of classifying him, would have been absurd, especially when I have mentioned a considerable number of much less distinguished thinkers'.[12]

Immediate acclaim is not necessarily a sound criterion as to the true value of the thought of a philosopher. Newman himself, referring to this phenomenon, remarked:

> If there be a subject, in which one is removed from the temptation of writing for popularity etc it is this, for if there is any thing at once new and good, years must elapse, the writer must be long dead, before it is acknowledged and received.[13]

He was well aware that considerable time might have to pass before he was correctly understood and appreciated as a philosopher. Referring to his *Grammar* in particular he wrote:

> As yet neither I nor any one else can say what is the worth of my argument or theory ... till time goes on for thinking men to understand its bearings, what are its merits and what its difficulties and defects, no criticism is worth any thing.[14]

The passage of time allows for a more objective view to be formed regarding the significance and influence of an individual philosopher. As the years go by it is easier to have a more universal vision of the overall development of philosophical thought. This enables us to judge the real significance and appropriate place for a particular philosopher to occupy in history. I believe that this is the case with Newman. It is only in the past few decades that the value of his thought has begun to be appreciated in the light of the subsequent trends in philosophy that appeared after his lifetime. In this context Copleston remarked that: 'The growth of interest in his philosophical thought ... has coincided with the spread of movements in philosophy ... which, on our looking back, are seen to have certain affinities with elements in Newman's reflections.'[15]

The Beginnings

Philosophy played a major role in Newman's education when he went up to Trinity College of Oxford University in June 1817. Three years later he took his Bachelor of Arts Degree in Classics and Mathematics in which he did not excel.[16] As an undergraduate he studied the three set books of Aristotle, *Rhetoric*, *Poetics* and *Nicomachean Ethics*. In the course of the following two years after graduation he continued his study of Aristotle along with many other interests in the fields of mineralogy, chemistry, musical composition and natural philosophy.[17] In 1821 he published his first paper, *On the Analogous Nature of the Difficulties in Mathematics and Those of Religion*, which clearly showed the influence of Aristotle's thought.[18]

After winning a fellowship at Oriel College in April 1822 his career in the academic world of Oxford began to flourish. His election as a fellow at twenty-one years of age, after a less than brilliant degree in the schools, brought him to the attention of Dr Richard Whately (1787–1863). He was also a fellow of Oriel and at this time was fully engaged in the revival of Aristotelian philosophy, particularly in the field of logic.[19] Whately belonged to the ranks of other British thinkers of the time like George Boole (1815–1864), Augustus De Morgan (1806–1871) and John Stuart Mill (1806–1873). Boole, the mathematician, was busy applying the methods of algebra to logic. De Morgan, mathematician and logician who worked with Boole, was investigating the existence of other forms of algebra other than that which dealt with real numbers. In 1860 De Morgan praised

Whately as being the restorer of the study of logic in the English language. In the introduction to his famous work, *A System of Logic, Ratiocinative and Inductive*, Mill also acknowledged the work of Whately as, 'a writer who has done more than any other person to restore this study to the rank from which it had fallen in the estimation of the cultivated class in our own country'.[20]

Although Newman had read *Artis Logicae Rudimenta* by Henry Aldrich for his BA examination it was from Whately that he learnt formal logic. As pointed out by Sillem, their friendship was based largely on their mutual admiration for the logic of Aristotle.[21] He collaborated with Whately in the writing of his celebrated work, *The Elements of Logic*, published in 1826. This consisted in compiling a synopsis of Whately's *Analytical Dialogues* and the incorporation of some of his own essays.[22] In the preface Whately made special mention of Newman's contribution: 'I cannot avoid particularizing the Rev. J. Newman ... who actually composed a considerable portion of the work as it now stands, from manuscripts not designed for publication, and who is the original author of several pages.'[23]

His first six years of association with Whately at Oriel were fruitful.[24] Under his tutelage he became more self-confident, grew in the ability to analyse critically and acquired a more universal outlook. It broadened his interests into new fields such as history, science, mathematics and Hebrew. He learnt how to make an exhaustive and thoroughly objective analysis of all the evidence that might be relevant in the discussion of any problem. This became a characteristic of his approach.

At the same time, however, Newman became critical of what he saw as a mechanical uniformity that Whately and his colleagues tried to impose on all reasoning. He was not happy with their tendency to consider progress in the development of ideas as following the path of formal logic. That is to say, to reduce our ways of reasoning to deductive or mathematical forms with little appreciation for a more inductive approach. Whately's *Elements of Logic* is itself a typical example of this way of thinking.[25]

He also became aware that his collaboration with Whately was having a certain negative effect on him. Later, commenting on this period of his life, he wrote: 'I was beginning to prefer intellectual excellence to moral; I was drifting in the direction of the Liberalism of the day.'[26] This tendency could have led him in any one of several directions. It could have ended in some form of rationalism, romanticism or simply scepticism. This negative aspect of their relationship, combined with a difference in character, caused Newman to gradually move away from Whately's sphere of influence. By 1831 the break was definitive.[27]

It was during the long vacation of 1818 that Newman became acquainted with the thought of John Locke. This was when he read for the first time his influential *Essay Concerning Human Understanding*.[28] Locke is arguably the first philosopher of note to have devoted the greater part of his philosophical career to producing a treatise on the nature of our reasoning processes. It is partly due to his efforts that we owe the importance that is now given to the theory of knowledge in philosophy. Newman seems to have been impressed by the matter-of-fact approach of this moderate empiricist to the science of knowing. In the thought of Locke he found both the strength and weakness of empiricism.[29] Nevertheless, while having respect for his way of thinking, he did not regard him as a philosophical ally. Many years later, when he came to write his *Grammar*, he chose Locke as one of his representatives of the kind of liberal rationalism in philosophy to which he was opposed. He discusses aspects of Locke's theories in contrast with his own thought. For example, Locke maintained the view that our intellectual assent to a proposition, from a subjective point of view, was susceptible to degrees of certainty. Newman, on the other hand, shows that when we give our act of assent we do so in an unconditional way.

There is evidence to show that Newman was familiar with the thought of Abraham Tucker (1705–1774) through reading *The Light of Nature Pursued*, the title given to some of his writings that were published posthumously. Tucker was one of the main proponents of the theories of association in psychology which came to the fore towards the latter half of the eighteenth century. Newman probably learnt more about his ideas from the work of

William Paley (1743–1805) who was an admirer of Tucker. Fundamental to these theories was that an association of images occurred spontaneously and unconsciously in the ordinary function of the human imagination which, when combined with the faculty of cognition, enabled us to acquire, as we grow in our experience of reality, an ever deeper insight into its nature. Although such notions are found in the thought of Aristotle it is possible that Newman's familiarity with Tucker's theories of association may have aided him in developing his own thought in this area. They may also have helped to confirm in him the great importance that he gave to the unity of all the potencies of the mind, including the imagination and memory, with respect to the whole cognitive process. However, there is no evidence to suggest that he was unduly influenced by such theories. It is more likely, as Sillem suggests, that it was a case of finding that these ideas concurred with his own experience.[30]

There are also some grounds for concluding that he had some knowledge of the so-called common sense school of Thomas Reid (1710–1796) and Dugald Stewart (1753–1828).[31] For example, Newman valued the common experience of mankind as constituting a certain safeguard against a possible idealism arising from basing a philosophy solely on personal experience.[32]

As he had done with Locke, Newman took some interest in the thought of John Stuart Mill as being another exponent of the intellectual liberalism of the day.[33] He was a philosopher of the utilitarian movement and was mainly interested in political theory and economics. In 1843 he published his famous book, *A System of Logic, Ratiocinative and Inductive*, which followed the empirical tradition of Locke. Subsequently this treatise eclipsed *The Elements of Logic* by Whately as the accepted doctrine on science and logic at Oxford. Newman read and made commentaries on this influential work of Mill in 1857.[34] It enabled him to become more familiar with the then current theories of the mathematical-physical sciences which he later makes use of in his *Grammar*.

As we have just seen, like many others who at this time received their education at the University of Oxford, his philosophical mind was nurtured within the Aristotelian tradition. His writings provide ample witness of his profound respect and understanding of the thought of Aristotle, 'the great philosopher of antiquity'.[35] Discussing the ability of the human intellect to acquire knowledge Newman said:

> While we are men, we cannot help, to a great extent, being Aristotelians, for the great Master does but analyze the thoughts, feelings, views, and opinions of human kind ... In many subject-matters, to think correctly, is to think like Aristotle; and we are his disciples whether we will or no, though we may not know it.[36]

He praised his logic in the following terms: 'The boldest, simplest, and most comprehensive theory which has been invented for the analysis of the reasoning process, is the well-known science for which we are indebted to Aristotle.'[37] Artz notices that in the *Grammar* alone he refers to Aristotle in one way or another some twenty-two times.[38] On one such occasion he proclaims: 'As to the intellectual position from which I have contemplated the subject, Aristotle has been my master.'[39] However, in spite of this great respect, only on rare occasions in the *Grammar* does he explicitly appeal to a particular aspect of Aristotle's thought in support of his own. The most significant instance of this is when he discusses the Illative Sense. In a later chapter I consider this example in detail.

Unfortunately, Newman has not left us any written commentary or discussion on Aristotle's fundamental concepts, such as being, substance and accidents, matter and form, or potency and act. Naturally this cannot be taken as implying that he accepted his thought uncritically. On one occasion in the *Grammar* he openly questions what he understands as the thought of Aristotle. He considered that Aristotle took too narrow a view on our reasoning, considering it only as an instrumental art.[40] We will see later that Newman emphasizes the personal nature of our acts of cognition, and shows that they are far more complex than his perception of Aristotle's view. The acquisition of knowledge involves the whole knowing subject as a person. The subsequent expression of that reasoning, 'paper logic' as Newman liked to call it, served only as a guide for others towards the truth in question, or as a written record of having reached it.

The Theologian

Within his philosophical background we must also include the influences stemming from his theological studies that contributed to the development of his thought. Joseph Butler (1692–1752), the outstanding Anglican divine, was among the favourite authors of Whately. Butler's major work, *The Analogy of Religion, Natural and Revealed, to the Constitution and Course of Nature*, represented a cogent defence of the reasonableness of Christianity in reaction to the then current scepticism. Newman began to read Butler in 1825 as his work on Whately's treatise of logic was drawing to a close.[41] Louis Bouyer affirms that one conclusion which he derived from his study of Butler was that any religion based solely on sentiment was not tenable.[42] In his *Apologia* he describes what he learnt from Butler's *Analogy*:

> If I may attempt to determine what I most gained from it, it lay in two points, ... they are the underlying principles of a great portion of my teaching. First, the very idea of an analogy between the separate works of God leads to the conclusion that the system which is of less importance is economically or sacramentally connected with the more momentous system, ... Secondly, Butler's doctrine that Probability is the guide of life, led me, ... to the question of the logical cogency of the Faith, on which I have written so much.[43]

Butler argued that, if we accept the premise that God is both the creator of the natural order and of the supernatural, then we must also accept that there are analogical similarities between these two dimensions of reality. For example, since we find problems in our scientific explanations of natural phenomena we should not be surprised to encounter some difficulties in our understanding of revealed truths. However, the problems we encounter in our rational knowledge do not, as a consequence, make us reject it all as a whole. On the grounds of the analogy between the two dimensions we should approach Christianity in the same way, and not reject it simply because we have come up against some intellectual anomalies. Butler's explanation of this analogy confirmed what Newman had thought since his youth, that physical reality forms part of a sacramental system which is an active and living witness of the supernatural dimension.[44] He used this principle to explain how everything that takes place in the natural order is linked with God's providential plans for the lives of individuals. It is important to bear in mind, as Sillem and Copleston observe, this theocentric approach present in Newman's thinking in order to fully appreciate his philosophy.[45]

In his *Analogy* Butler continued his argument showing that much of our natural knowledge is based on probability, that 'probability is the guide to life'.[46] This leads him to the conclusion that, when this notion is seen in the light of his original analogy, it shows that we should give great value to the accumulative evidence for Christianity.

Newman was happy to accept that probability was a practical rule of common sense in everyday life. However, he was critical of Butler's way of understanding its nature in the context of the operations of the intellect. Butler claimed that, while the conclusions of demonstrative reasoning were certain, those based on probability were subject to degrees of certainty. Newman did not agree and, as we shall see later, shows that intellectual assent, by its nature, is given unconditionally. From his writings it is clear that he had great respect for the thought of Butler. At the same time, however, it is equally apparent that he only makes use of his ideas in as much as they concur with his own experience and way of thinking.[47]

Newman scholars agree that the greatest influence on the development of his philosophical mind derived from theological sources came from his profound knowledge of the Early Fathers of the Church.[48] It was during the long vacation of 1828 that he began a systematic reading of their writings, especially of the Alexandrians. This gave him a certain familiarity with the philosophy of Plato, and subsequent neo-platonic thinking, as viewed by these Christian writers. The beginnings of his theory on the development of ideas, both in philosophy and theology, can be traced to these roots.[49] Nevertheless, it is worth noting that in Newman's writings there is no mention or discussion of either the philosophy of Plato or of any of the neo-platonists.

The study of Butler and the Church Fathers enriched Newman's thinking in the early part of his university career. Later in his life there were also other influences. These came as a result of his theological pursuits after becoming a Roman Catholic in 1845. From this time onwards he became acquainted with the more dominant trends in philosophy and theology then present in Catholic academic circles, especially during his sojourn in Rome. I feel that on occasions these aspects, which certainly contributed to the maturing of his philosophical thought, are not given sufficient importance by Newman scholars.

From November 1846 to May 1847 he attended the Pontifical College of *Propaganda Fídei* in Rome. At the time this was the educational institution of the Catholic Church that provided the necessary training for priests destined for missionary countries. It was here that he came into contact with eminent scholastic theologians of the time, such as Giovanni Perrone (1794–1876) and Carlo Passaglia (1814–1887). Perrone was then teaching at the Pontifical Gregorian University in Rome. It was under his supervision that Newman wrote a theological paper on the development of Christian doctrine.[50] He was disappointed with what he found in Catholic academic circles regarding philosophy. He wrote in a letter: 'Aristotle is in no favour here – no, not in Rome – nor St. Thomas. I have read Aristotle and St. Thomas and owe a great deal to them, but they are out of favour here and throughout Italy.'[51]

He possessed a complete collection of the works of St Thomas Aquinas from the time he was a Fellow at Oriel College. There is evidence to suggest that he read at least some parts of them during this period. Sillem notes that his contact with the current scholastic tradition of philosophy and theology while in Rome enabled him to become more familiar with the thought of Aquinas.[52] On the other hand, the strictly logical approach of nineteenth-century scholasticism was not congenial to his way of thinking.[53] Nevertheless, he acknowledged it as forming part of the theological tradition of the Catholic Church, and its role in the development of Catholic theology.[54] I do not think it idle speculation to consider that Newman's thought might have been profoundly enriched had his time in Rome enabled him to know the authentic teaching of Aquinas. As just mentioned, he was disillusioned by what he thought to be a rather superficial approach to philosophy among the scholars he met. Witness to his great esteem for Aquinas is clearly shown in the many references to him found in his writings, occasionally placing him within the ranks of the Fathers of the Church.[55] For instance, in his *Apologia* he describes Catholic theology in the following terms:

> Catholic inquiry has taken certain definite shapes, and has thrown itself into the form of a science, with a method and a phraseology of its own, under the intellectual handling of great minds, such as St Athanasius, St Augustine and St Thomas; and I feel no temptation at all to break in pieces the great legacy of thought thus committed to us for these latter days.[56]

It is clear that Newman was no disciple of Aquinas, for the simple reason that he did not know his philosophy in any great depth. Consequently, as Collins also observes, we must conclude that the thought of Aquinas played little part in Newman's approach to philosophy.[57] In the text of his *Grammar* he does not refer once to Aquinas. Nevertheless, it must not be forgotten that their philosophies shared some of the same sources. Henry Tristam remarks that they both had the same profound respect for the thought of Aristotle and the Fathers of the Church.[58]

The Scientist

Newman, together with his interests in philosophy and theology during his early years at Oxford, was also attracted to mathematics and physics.[59] For his Bachelor's degree he read mathematics as well as classics. After winning his fellowship to Oriel he pursued his liking for mathematics.[60] Combined with his research for Whately it could be argued that he was also part of the then current movement for the revival of the study of mathematics at Oxford. He took a special interest in the French analytical school of mathematics and was familiar with the work of Joseph Louis Lagrange (1736–1813), Pierre Simon Laplace (1749–1827) and Augustin Louis Cauchy (1789–1857).[61]

In the field of physics he appreciated the thought of Francis Bacon (1561–1626), 'Our own English philosopher', and mentions him frequently in his writings.[62] He considered Bacon to be an early precursor of Newtonian physics, a pioneer of the experimental sciences and among the first to advocate the method of scientific induction. In his *Grammar* he refers to Bacon's view on the uniformity of the laws of nature in support of his own understanding of the cognitive process.[63]

Newman was also an admirer of the renowned British physicist Isaac Newton (1642–1727), as can be gathered by the many references to him.[64] It will be remembered that Newton, among other discoveries, gained his fame from having formulated the law of gravity and what have become known as the three laws of motion. In his *Grammar* he shows his esteem by attributing to him what he calls, 'the method of proof which is the foundation of modern mathematical science'.[65] He is referring to that branch of mathematics now known as differential calculus. He makes use of this 'method' in his explanation of Informal Inference. In a later chapter I deal with this mathematical model in detail. It is clear that his various scientific interests added a valuable dimension to his philosophical thought and appreciation of reality.

Originality

While acknowledging the primordial role that the thought of
Aristotle played in the formation of Newman's philosophical
mind it is important to stress that he was not dominated by any
single influence. He did not follow any of the philosophical
schools in vogue at the time. As has been remarked earlier, this
is probably one of the major factors hindering his recognition as
a significant philosopher. Scholars in general agree that he was
a man of exceptional independence of mind.[66] In this context
Gilson affirms that he 'did not write as a disciple of the scholastic masters whose works illustrated the thirteenth century; he
wrote in the free style of a twelfth-century master, full of classical erudition'.[67]

He was well aware that he did not conform to the philosophical trends of the day. In a draft preface for an edition of
the *Grammar*, which in the event was not published, he stated
that he had neither 'recognised the tenets nor the language of
existing schools of thought', and wished to 'speak for
himself'.[68] On the other hand, in order to clarify his own view,
he was happy to compare or contrast his thought with that of
other thinkers. Only on comparatively rare occasions does he
explicitly refer to other philosophers in support of his own
conclusions. He writes with a freshness of someone who has
mastered his sources, and thinks his subject through with great
diligence and scientific rigour.

His originality has proved to be a cause of misunderstanding.
Even before the publication of his *Grammar* he received criticism from one of the leading scholastic philosophers of the time.
He had asked Charles Meynell to review some of his work. He
was somewhat dismayed at being told that what he had written
corresponded to a position of 'hypothetical realism'.[69] The
implication was that it could be interpreted as a form of idealism. This was a rather odd criticism. Even a casual acquaintance
with his writings shows that any form of idealism is completely
alien to Newman's philosophy. Nowhere do we find any attempt
to subjugate reality with thought, or to enclose it within a logical
system. His approach is to use the intellect to explore, to get to

know the depth and beauty of that reality of which we form part. As suggested by Wilfred P. Ward, I think that such a criticism was the result of trying to fit Newman's thought into some kind of scholastic mould.[70] He did not follow any particular school of philosophy, least of all that of the then current form of scholasticism.

It seems to me that when Newman's philosophy is tackled by unfriendly critics they are sometimes tempted to impose their own prejudices. These can form a barrier that makes it difficult for them to penetrate the depth of his view. It can lead them to being rather quick to dismiss, or condemn, what they do not fully comprehend. Alternatively, friendly commentators sometimes run the risk of not discovering his genuine thought in their haste to see in it the reflection of their own cherished ideas. Those who wish to appreciate his philosophy must approach his thought with a truly open mind, being prepared to find originality that must be considered first of all in its own right, and not judged solely according to the criteria of another way of thinking.

In conclusion we can say that, first and foremost, Newman's philosophical background must be situated within the context of the Aristotelian tradition then present in the University of Oxford. To this we have to add what he derived from the then current atmosphere of British empiricism, and in particular what he learnt from Locke, Whately and Mill. At the same time the various less direct influences should also be borne in mind. I refer to those stemming from both his theological and scientific interests. In this respect I think, along with Copleston and Collins, that special mention must be made of his appreciation for Butler, his profound knowledge of the Church Fathers and for the thought of Newton.[71]

John Henry Newman has made his mark in history as a great theologian. Like Aquinas, as A. Dwight Culler also remarks, he appreciated the importance of basing theology on a firm philosophical foundation, while at the same time being fully aware of the differences between these two sciences.[72] It is the *Grammar of Assent* that, from among all his works, exhibits this characteristic most clearly. His theological argument rests on a solid philosophical bedrock. However, his philosophy is clearly discerned from within this theological context. Furthermore, if we can show that what is original in Newman's thought is coherent with our understanding of reality, then it will form part of his contribution to the advance of philosophy. The following chapter examines the basic concepts of his approach to philosophy.

Notes

1. Pope John Paul II, Encyclical, *Fides et ratio* (14 September 1998), n. 74.
2. Sillem, p. 21; cf. ibid., pp. 149–250: Sillem describes Newman's philosophical background.
3. Gilson, 'Introduction', in *GA* (1955), pp. 20–1; cf. ibid., p. 9.
4. Cf. Lonergan, *Proceedings of the American Catholic Philosophical Society*, p. 257; *Collection. Papers by Bernard Lonergan*, p. ix; Tracy, pp. 91–2; Norris, pp. xix, 47, 82, 89, 149, 196, 208–9.
5. Walgrave, *Newman. Le développement du dogme*, p. 359.
6. Collins, pp. 1–2.
7. Cf. Copleston, vol. VIII, pp. 510–25.
8. Ker, 'Introduction', in *GA* (1985), p. lv.
9. Sillem, p. 248.
10. Artz, 'Newman as Philosopher', p. 287; cf. ibid., pp. 265, 272; Artz, 'Preface', in Norris, pp. xi–xii.
11. Sillem, p. 250.
12. Copleston, vol. VIII, *Preface*, p. x; cf. Sillem, pp. 75–6.
13. *Phil N* II, p. 86.
14. *LD* XXV, p. 128; cf. ibid., p. 126.
15. Copleston, vol. VIII, pp. 524–5.
16. Cf. *AW*, p. 10.
17. Cf. *AW*, p. 55; Sillem, pp. 150–3.
18. This article was published in the *Christian Observer*, 6 March 1821, cf. Willam, *Aristolelische Erkenntuislehre bei Whately und Newman*, p. 142.
19. Cf. *AW*, pp. 10–66.
20. Mill, p. 2.
21. Cf. Sillem, pp. 153–4, 157, 159.
22. Cf. *Apo*, pp. 8, 11; *AW*, pp. 10, 67.
23. Whately, *The Elements of Logic*, p. viii.

24. Cf. *Apo*, p. 11; *AW*, pp. 67–71; Sillem, p. 11; Chadwick, *From Bossuet to Newman*, pp. 111–12.
25. Cf. Whately, *The Elements of Logic*, pp. 207–9.
26. *Apo*, p. 14; cf. *AW*, pp. 69–70.
27. Cf. *LD* XIV, p. 385; *Apo*, pp. 11–13; Dessain, *John Henry Newman*, p. 8.
28. Cf. *AW*, p. 40.
29. Cf. *Idea*, pp. 158–60, 163, 319.
30. Cf. Sillem, pp. 203–20.
31. Cf. Copleston, vol. V, pp. 364–73, 375–83; Artz, 'Newman as Philosopher', p. 273; Flanagan, p. 108.
32. Cf. Copleston, vol. V, p. 273.
33. Cf. Cameron, 'Newman and the Empiricist Tradition', pp. 91–2.
34. Cf. *TP* I, pp. 39–47.
35. *GA*, p. 221 (342); cf. ibid., pp. 220 (341), 228–9 (354–5), 266–7 (414–15), 277 (430); *Idea*, pp. xiii, 6, 52, 53, 54, 77–8, 101, 106, 109, 134, 265, 275, 280, 283, 383, 431, 470, 669; *US*, p. 258. For an account of Aristotle's influence on Newman, cf. Willam, *Aristotelische Erkenntuislehre bei Whately und Newman*; ibid., 'Die philosophischen Grundpositionen Newmans', in *Newman-Studiun* III, pp.111–56; ibid., 'Aristotelische Bausteine der Entwicklungstheorie Newmans', in *Newman-Studien* VI, pp. 193–226.
36. *Idea*, pp. 109–10.
37. *US*, p. 258.
38. Cf. Artz, 'Newman as Philosopher', p. 268.
39. *GA*, p. 277 (430).
40. Cf. *GA*, p. 210 (338).
41. Cf. *Apo*, pp. 10–11; *AW*, p. 78.
42. Cf. Bouyer, pp. 71–3; Ward, vol. I, p. 38.
43. *Apo*, pp. 10–11; cf. ibid., pp. 22–3, 105–6, 108.
44. Cf. *US*, p. 286; *PS* I, pp. 18–20; *SE* II, pp. 180–3; *GA*, pp. 246 (382), 319–21 (496–8).
45. Cf. Sillem, pp. 174–5; Copleston, vol. VIII, p. 513.
46. Butler, pp. 3, 236.
47. Cf. *US*, p. 286; *Dev*, pp. 50, 63–4, 71, 74, 75, 103–4; *Idea*, pp. 61, 100, 158, 226, 319; *GA*, pp. 207 (319–20), 208 (321–2), 222–3 (344), 246 (382); Sillem, pp. 179, 180–1; Chadwick, pp. 86–95; De Smet, pp. 21–38.
48. Cf. Sillem, pp. 181–3; Gilson, 'Introduction', in *GA* (1955), pp. 17–18; Norris, pp. 49–51, 152–5, 192–3, 200.

49. Cf. *Apo*, pp. 110, 127–9; Walgrave, *Newman. Le développement du dogme*, pp. 23–7.
50. Cf. Newman, *Gregorianum*.
51. Letter to J. D. Dalgairns quoted in Ward, vol. I, p. 166.
52. Cf. Sillem, pp. 234–40.
53. Cf. *Diff* II, p. 24.
54. Cf. *HS* II, p. 475.
55. Cf. *Idea*, pp. 134, 263–4, 354, 384, 431, 470; *HS* II, p. 226; *SE*, p. 55; *TP* I, p. 34; *Diff* II, pp. 246–7, 256; *PN* II, pp. 101, 104, 162, 177–9; *Mix*, p. 99; *Prepos*, p. 306; *GA*, pp. 323–4 (503); Ward, vol. II, pp. 501–2.
56. *Apo*, p. 251.
57. Cf. Collins, p. 16.
58. Cf. Tristam, 'Introduction', in Flanagan, pp. ix–x; *Idea*, pp. 431, 470.
59. Cf. *AW*, pp. 44, 55.
60. Cf. *AW*, p. 61; Sillem, pp. 183–8.
61. Cf. Culler, pp. 80–1.
62. *GA*, p. 226 (350); cf. ibid., pp. 233 (361), 239 (372); *Dev*, pp. 110–13; *Idea*, pp. x, xiii, xiv, 74–5, 77, 90, 113, 118–19, 175, 220, 221–2, 263, 319, 437, 442, 444, 446, 447, 448; *US*, pp. 205–7.
63. Cf. *GA*, p. 226 (350).
64. Cf. *US*, p. 217; *Dev*, p. 101; *Idea*, pp. xiii, 49, 53, 134, 304, 324, 460; *GA*, pp. 150 (230), 193 (298), 207 (320), 219 (339), 219 (340), 220 (341).
65. *GA*, p. 207 (320).
66. Cf. Sillem, p. 238; Walgrave, *Newman. Le développement du dogme*, p. 19; Flanagan, p. 109; Copleston, vol. VIII, p. 513.
67. Gilson, 'Introduction', in *GA* (1955), p. 18.
68. Newman, *OA*, 2.2, manuscript dated December 1868, quoted by Ker, 'Introduction', in *GA* (1985), pp. xliii–xliv; cf. *LD* XXV, p. 36.
69. *LD* XXIV, p. 306; cf. ibid., p. 312.
70. Cf. Ward, vol. II, pp. 268–70.
71. Cf. Copleston, vol. VIII, pp. 512–13; Collins, p. 4.
72. Cf. Culler, pp. 269–70; *Dev*, pp. 336–8; *Idea*, pp. 25–9, 52–3, 60–6.

CHAPTER 2

FOUNDATIONS

The *Grammar of Assent* is the primary source for Newman's philosophy. However, as observed by Dessain and Ker, it was not his intention to write it in the form of a systematic treatise.[1] Consequently, in order to facilitate the understanding of his approach to philosophy it is helpful to establish what might be considered as his foundational concepts. The importance of doing this is even more apparent when it is remembered that he was an independent thinker, and did not form part of any recognized philosophical trend or school. This foundation will provide us with an appropriate context within which to consider his theory of knowledge.

Realist

The general agreement among scholars testifies to Newman's philosophical position as being that of a realist.[2] Dessain affirms that 'if he must be given a label, he was a moderate realist', and even goes on to claim that he followed the realism of Aquinas.[3] Sillem echoes this conclusion when he says that, 'I see him as coming down in favour of Moderate Realism'.[4]

According to the accepted designations given to realist philosophers the most appropriate for Newman would appear to be that of a moderate realist. However, it seems clear to me that he himself would be quite happy with being simply referred to as a realist. All his writings touching on philosophical topics bear testimony to a consistent realist approach. He accepts without reservations the objective existence of reality as independent from the knowing subject. In one of his *University Sermons* of 1839 he says: 'We are surrounded by beings which exist quite independently of us – exist whether we exist, or cease to exist, whether we have cognizance of them or no.'[5] In another sermon of the same year he proposes: 'Let us take things as we find them: let us not attempt to distort them into what they are not. True philosophy deals with facts. We cannot make facts. All our wishing cannot change them. We must use them.'[6] His *Grammar* is replete with statements of realism, and even appears to reiterate the same conclusion from this *Sermon*: 'We are in a world of facts, and we use them; for there is nothing else to use. We do not quarrel with them, but we take them as they are, and avail ourselves of what they can do for us.'[7] As Sillem comments, he considered philosophical reflection as the way to know reality, 'and not as a means for constructing an abstract system of ideas'.[8]

Newman follows Aristotle in considering our experience of reality as the source from which all our knowledge is derived: 'The senses, then, are the only instruments which we know to be granted to us for direct and immediate acquaintance with things external to us.'[9] In a note to the 1871 edition of his *University Sermons* he expresses his understanding of the direct contact that we have with reality through our senses in the following terms:

> The senses convey to the mind 'substantial truth', in so far as they bring home to us that certain things are, and *in confuso* what they are. But has a man born blind, by means of having smelling, taste and touch, such an idea of physical nature, as may be called *substantially* true or, on the contrary, an idea which at best is but the *shadow* of the truth? for, in whichever respect, whether as in substance or by a shadow, the blind man knows the objects of sight.[10]

Within the context of our ability to know reality he includes the knowledge of our inner reality: 'By our self consciousness we know about ourselves.'[11]

In his writings there is no discussion on what is generally referred to as the metaphysics of being. However, I would agree with Boekraad in saying that it seems to be present in an implicit way in his philosophy.[12] His approach is entirely consistent with the acceptance of the self-evident truth that the intellect's first apprehension of reality, in the metaphysical sense, is that of being. In fact, as we shall see, he gives this truth pride of place when he discusses self-evident truths in his *Grammar*.

When it comes to describing the beings which constitute reality he does not use any particular terminology in the *Grammar*. This would imply that, although using different words, he does not intend to make any particular philosophical distinction between them. He uses expressions such as: 'things',[13] 'real things',[14] 'real being',[15] 'unit realities',[16] 'individual being',[17] 'the particular',[18] 'concrete facts',[19] 'the concrete',[20] 'concrete matters'[21] and 'concrete reality'.[22]

He considers that the role of the philosopher is to accept reality and then to proceed to contemplate it, to investigate its causes and nature. Possibly the closest he comes to giving us a definition of philosophy is in one of his sermons preached in 1841 where he says:

> Philosophy, then, is Reason exercised upon Knowledge; or the Knowledge not merely of things in general, but of things in their relations to one another. It is the power of referring every thing to its true place in the universal system, – of understanding the various aspects of each of its parts, – of comprehending the exact value of each, – of tracing each backwards to its beginning, and forward to its end, ... and thus of accounting for anomalies, answering objections, supplying deficiencies, making allowance for errors, and meeting emergencies.[23]

Some twenty years later, in 1863, he had the following to say about philosophy:

> Next, the philosopher's conceptions are almost as bold and excursive as the poet's. He has especial need of a large mind.

He demands and exercises liberty of thought within the bounds of experience. He has the power of a boundless speculation, which he carries on by his originality in abstracting, generalizing, and applying.[24]

Newman's thought on self-evident truths and first principles gives us a clear insight into his realist approach to philosophy. Several pages of the *Grammar* are dedicated to this topic. He discusses them within the context of 'Presumption'. This is one of his classifications of the various kinds of Notional Assents. He describes self-evident truths as 'abstractions to which we give a notional assent in consequence of our particular experiences of qualities in the concrete, to which we give a real assent'.[25] His distinction between Real and Notional Assent will be dealt with in a later chapter. At this juncture it will suffice to note that by Real Assent he is referring to our act of Assent to a proposition that relates to a concrete individual being in reality. On the other hand, a Notional Assent refers to those 'made to propositions which express abstractions or notions'.[26] In other words, he is referring to our Assents to propositions that imply intellectual abstraction from sense knowledge; they are the result of the intellect's ability to abstract the essences of beings from the singular beings: 'to elevate our experience into something more than it is in itself'.[27] That is to say, he understands self-evident truths as derived from intellectual abstraction followed by Notional Assent. They are not just the result of our observation of empirical generalizations as proposed by the empiricists.

They are neither a priori ideas, nor hypothetical premises, that might then be employed to construct a purely logical system, perfectly idealistic. They are the fundamental truths of reality:

The recondite sources of all knowledge, as to which logic provides no common measure of minds, – which are accepted by some, rejected by others, – in which, and not in the syllogistic exhibitions, lies the whole problem of attaining to truth, – and which are called self-evident by their respective advocates because they are evident in no other way.[28]

A self-evident truth or first principle is the 'proposition with which we start in reasoning on any given subject matter'.[29] They form the premises for our inferences, the beginning and points of reference for all our reasoning:

> They are our guides and standards in speculating, reasoning, judging, deliberating, deciding, and acting: they are to the mind what the circulation of the blood and the various functions of our animal organs are to the body. They are the conditions of our mental life; by them we form our view of events, of deeds, of persons, of lines of conduct, of aims, of moral qualities, of religions. They constitute the difference between man and man; they characterize him.[30]

When he refers to the ability of the intellect to attain such truths he uses the term 'intuition'.[31] In some notes of 1853 he carefully distinguishes, with a nota bene, between intuition and the process of reasoning: 'NB. In *intuition* the light is in the proposition itself – in *demonstration* the light is thrown upon the proposition from surrounding already known truths.'[32]

His most extensive discussion of intuition is found in a paper written about 1860 with the title, *Assent and Intuition*. This essay deals with the subject in a rather phenomenological way considering all its possible meanings and implications. Within the semantic range of intuition he includes the sense that Aristotle gave to the term induction. He begins with a definition: 'When the assent which I give to a truth, ... is simple and absolute, I shall call it an *intuition*, as being an insight into things as they are.'[33] Later in this paper he expands on his definition, and even hints that its operation, as an act of the intellect, is possibly due to a certain participation of being which exists between the knowing mind and reality:

> The direct insight which I personally possess (so far forth) into things as they are. In other words, it is the vision, analogous to eye-sight, which my intellectual nature has of things as they are, arising from the original, elementary sympathy or harmony between myself and what is external to myself, I and

it being portions of one whole, and, in a certain sense, existing for each other.[34]

Newman was accused publicly by Andrew Martin Fairbairn, in an article published in the *Contemporary Review* of May 1885, of philosophical scepticism. In his equally public answer, in the October issue of the same journal, he referred to intuition 'as being "the apprehension of first principles," and Aristotle has taught me to call it νοῦς, or the *noetic* faculty'.[35] It is clear that Newman recognizes the classical distinction, following the tradition of Aristotle and Aquinas, between *intellectus* and *ratio*.[36] That is to say, where the term reason (*ratio*) tends to be used to designate the discursive action of the intellect.

In his paper of 1860 he continues by saying that, although intuition is a power belonging to the nature of the intellect, the ability of its use varies from person to person. Thus intuitions need not be held universally in order for them to be true. He explains:

Intuition, though it is the absolute assent which we are naturally capable of giving to the first principles of all knowledge, may be exercised on other truths, it is the gift of the few as well as of the multitude. It is the exercise of a faculty, which is stronger or weaker in this man or that, but of which in every state truth is the object; nor is there any other limit to the number of possible intuitions, than that of the things on which thought can be employed. Those things which ordinarily are known by means of reasoning, may by some men be ascertained by intuition.[37]

An entry in his *Philosophical Notebook* mentions that time may be needed in order for the intellect to discern certain self-evident truths:

A continuous meditation may bring out to a particular mind a truth in the way of intuition, I mean as something perceived without reason or middle term – as eyes long accustomed to gaze upon darkness see objects for which others would require more light.[38]

In his paper he quotes Aristotle to show that, in our quest for knowledge in a certain field, we should give careful consideration to the conclusions of those who have had long experience in this same area:

> One should attend to the sayings and opinions of the experienced, the old, the wise, *though they be incapable of proof*, not less than to proofs; for they see the principles, in that they have *an eye* in consequence of their experience.[39]

His paper on intuition does not refer to the distinction, which is usually made by those following the school of Aristotle, between essential induction and empirical induction. Essential induction is the case where the intellect formulates a proposition on realizing that there is an essential and necessary link between the subject and predicate of a proposition. On the other hand, empirical induction is the scientific method whereby a general proposition is formulated as an explanation for a certain physical phenomenon. Such a conclusion is the result of the empirical observation of re-occurring individual physical phenomena when certain conditions are present. Empirical induction depends on the principle of causality for its verification. However, it refers to contingent causes, and consequently there is no implication of necessity in its conclusions as is proper to those of essential induction. In this respect Newman's paper is rather confusing. He gives the term intuition a very broad semantic range without making any specific distinctions with regard to its possible meanings. Nevertheless, he is aware of the distinction just mentioned. That is to say, he appreciates the difference between necessary and contingent causality. This is clear, for example, when he alerts us to the danger of attributing a false necessity to empirical induction. In such cases he calls them 'unreal intuitions', and says that they:

> Are commonly such as arise from giving to systems which are short of necessary, that authority which belongs only to what is necessary and eternal. For instance, I suppose many persons would call the laws of this physical universe, in

which we pass our lives, the nature of things; yet without sufficient reason.[40]

In other words, he recognizes the difference between essential and empirical induction without using this terminology.

Ten years later, in his *Grammar*, he expresses this distinction with more clarity. He restricts his use of the term intuition to designate the intellect's ability to discover self-evident truths or, in other words, to essential induction. Conversely, he identifies the term induction with empirical or scientific induction.

The first self-evident truth that he considers in the *Grammar* is the intellect's apprehension of reality as such. We know 'that there is an external world, and that all the phenomena of sense proceed from it'. He distinguishes between this truth, as apprehended by the rational being which transcends pure sense experience, and the simple instinctive awareness of the external world proper to other animals. He explains:

> What the human mind does is what brutes cannot do, viz. to draw from our ever-recurring experiences of its testimony in particulars a general proposition ... the great aphorism, that there is an external world, and that all the phenomena of sense proceed from it. This general proposition, to which we go on to assent, goes (*extensive*, though not *intensive*) far beyond our experience, illimitable as that experience may be, and represents a notion'.[41]

In the *Grammar* Newman gives a phenomenological description of the intuition of being by the human intellect. Put in simple metaphysical terms he is saying that the intellect is able to abstract from its knowledge of particular beings the universal concept of being. He also considers this self-evident truth as 'one of universal reception'. In this respect there does not seem to be anything in his writings to suggest that he is not in agreement with Aquinas.[42] That is to say, that the very first and most fundamental concept to be perceived by the human intellect is that of being, and that this is the foundation of our capacity to know reality.[43] For instance, in his *Philosophical Notebook* he comments:

In knowledge we begin with wholes, not with parts. We see the landscape, or the mountain, or the sky. We perceive men, each individually being a whole. Then we take to pieces, or take aspects of, this general and vague object, which is before us.[44]

In an entry of his *Philosophical Notebook* there is another example showing his awareness that our first intellectual apprehension is of being:

What is called reasoning then is in its essence not a deduction, but it is the perception of certain complex ideas, or the modes or the dress of things. Thought and being, or sensation and being, are brought home to me by one act of consciousness, prior to any exercise of ratiocination.[45]

He also expresses this self-evident truth in its propositional form known as the principle of non-contradiction: 'Truth is one and the same; a thing cannot be and not be' at the same time and under the same circumstances.[46]

The second self-evident truth that he discusses is that of 'the Ubiquitous Presence of One Supreme Master' of the universe.[47] He explains how this truth is arrived at through our continual experience, by means of our internal senses, of 'Conscience'. Just as our intellectual perception of reality is derived from our sense experience, so our apprehension of this second self-evident truth comes from our awareness of Conscience. Later in his *Grammar* he makes use of our experience of Conscience to show that it can lead us to making an Assent to the existence of God.[48] As both Walgrave and John Holloway point out, it is important to bear in mind the central role that Newman gives to divine providence in his philosophy.[49] He views reality within the context of a divine providence that is shown in the harmonious pattern within nature, and in God's 'guiding hand' that cares for mankind. This fundamental idea is echoed throughout his writings.[50] When applied to the human being he sees it as implying that our God given nature is endowed with the ability to know reality with certitude: 'It is He who teaches us all knowledge; and the way by which we acquire it is His way.'[51]

His review of self-evident truths in the *Grammar* continues with those 'expressed in such propositions as "There is a right and a wrong", "a true and a false", "a just and an unjust", "a beautiful and a deformed"'. As with the other self-evident truths these are:

> Conclusions or abstractions from particular experiences; and an assent to their existence is not an assent to things or their images, but to notions ... Such notions indeed are an evidence of the reality of the special sentiments in particular instances, ... But in themselves they are abstractions from facts.[52]

The last self-evident truth that he deals with is the principle of causality. He opens his discussion with what seems to be a rather disconcerting statement: 'It is to me a perplexity that grave authors seem to enumerate as an intuitive truth, that every thing must have a cause.'[53] From what follows it appears that his 'perplexity' is due to thinking that, if causality is defined in such an absolute way, then it seems to imply a contradiction with respect to the existence of the 'One, who is Himself without cause'. Unfortunately he neither names any of these 'grave authors', nor does he consider how they resolve such an apparent paradox. His explanation of causality begins with the evidence provided by the awareness that we have of our human acts, 'that nothing happens without a cause, is derived, in the first instance, from what we know of ourselves; and we argue analogically from what it is within us to what is external to us'. The 'notion of causation' as a self-evident truth originates from our knowledge of 'agents possessed of intelligence and will. It is the notion of power combined with a purpose and an end', and he continues:

> Since causation implies a sequence of acts in our own case, and our doing is always posterior, never contemporaneous or prior, to our willing, therefore, when we witness invariable antecedents and consequents, we call the former the cause of

the latter, though intelligence is absent, from the analogy of external appearances.[54]

That is to say, as a consequence of our experience of human acts we attribute, by analogy, the self-evident truth of causation to the external world of irrational nature. However, such a derivation of the principle of causality with respect to irrational nature would seem to contradict his definition of intuition. It seems to suggest that it cannot be a truth perceived immediately by our intellect through sense experience, but a truth derived by analogy with a prior self-evident truth. According to his explanation, found in notes of about 1860, this would then appear to correspond to what he designates as a '*contuition*' rather than intuition.[55] In his *Grammar* he does not introduce such a distinction.

However, later in his section on causality he does clearly imply that it is a self-evident truth when he says:

That on which a thing under given circumstances follows ... requires a discrimination and exactness of thought for its apprehension, which implies special mental training; else, how do we learn to call food the cause of refreshment, but day never the cause of night, though night follows day more surely than refreshment follows food?[56]

Although this statement could have been more explicit, the implication is clear. The intellect is able to recognize in a direct and immediate way cause and effect. That is to say, through our sense experience the intellect can detect aspects of reality, in this case causality, which are not given in the purely empirical observations or physical phenomena as such. The intellect apprehends that, within the myriad changes which we observe in reality, a certain coming into being is the result of a specific interaction of other beings, whether they are directed by human will or not. In other words, the intellect is able to distinguish, from among all the changes that we observe in reality, those that are causes and those that are effects. A cause is that which brings a being to be what it is now, but that was not present before a certain interaction took place, and this result of that cause we call its effect.

Newman concludes his first section on causality with a definition: 'I consider a cause to be an effective will; and, by the doctrine of causation, I mean the notion, or first principle, that all things come of effective will.' This statement seems to be an echo of Aristotle's concept of final cause.

He then turns his attention in the *Grammar* to causality in the sense of 'an ordinary succession of antecedents and consequents, or what is called the Order of Nature', and affirms that it is 'another first principle or notion, derived by us from experience'. He further clarifies that: 'By natural law I mean the fact that things happen uniformly according to fixed circumstances, and not without them or at random: that is, that they happen in an order.'[57] However, he is careful to add: 'the order of nature is not necessary, but general in its manifestations'.[58] Elsewhere in his *Grammar* he reiterates this conclusion: 'General laws are not inviolable truths; much less are they necessary causes' which exclude the occurrence of exceptions.[59] It is clear that he has in mind David Hume's argument against the possibility of miracles based on the presumption of a necessity inherent in the laws of nature.[60] Newman explains that, since the order in the universe is caused by the 'Will' of God, therefore: 'That which willed it, can unwill it; and the invariableness of law depends on the unchangeableness of that Will.' He concludes: 'as a cause implies a will, so order implies a purpose'. In the 'Order of Nature', as a self-evident truth, he recognizes the ultimate 'final cause', and he proceeds to refer to God as 'Mind', written with a capital letter, reminiscent of Aristotle's terminology. When dealing with this topic in some of his other writings he does distinguish between the concept of design in the universe and that of order in relation to the First Cause.[61]

In the *Grammar*, as we have just seen, he includes 'the Order of Nature' among his self-evident truths. However, it is interesting to note that some years previously he had expressed some doubt about this. In 1861, referring to 'the stability of the laws of nature' as an intuition he remarked that: 'I do not think it immediate.'[62] This reminds us of what has already been touched on earlier, that Newman preferred to use his term '*contuition*' to refer to our intellectual knowledge of the principle of causality.

A cursory comparison with the thought of Aquinas on this topic shows that Newman's view is both incomplete and rather confusing. Jaki even goes so far as to say that it is prone to an empiricist interpretation.[63] This can hardly be true since he does clearly acknowledge the role of the intellect in perceiving cause and effect. The observation of causality is not just the result of empirical generalizations. Unfortunately, apart from the *Grammar* we do not find any further discussion on this topic in his writings. There are only some passing references.[64] For instance, he criticizes Mill for his denial of 'efficient causation'.[65]

Since Newman never explicitly proposed, at least in writing, a metaphysics of being it would be unfair to criticize him too harshly for his lack of metaphysical precision and completeness regarding causality. However, we can speculate that, had he been aware of the basic insight of Aquinas on this topic, then his phenomenological approach to it would have benefited greatly. That is to say, if he had understood causation as the dynamic counterpart of the universal participation of being within reality. Causality is the intellectual apprehension of change in terms of the participation of being in the Being, the 'one who is Himself without cause', and from whom is derived all causality.[66] Such an insight would have helped Newman to view God as the First Cause and all other causes as secondary. Furthermore, it would have enabled him to distinguish between necessary, contingent and free causes. It is quite clear, however, that he is aware of these distinctions. For example, when discussing the differences between the sciences of theology and physics he refers to 'final' and 'first cause', 'final causes' and 'physical causes'.[67] By the latter, from the context, he implies contingent causes.

From very early in his career he appreciated the fundamental importance of self-evident truths. In one of his *University Sermons*, preached in 1839, he tells us:

Half the controversies in the world are verbal ones; and could they be brought to a plain issue, they would be brought to a prompt termination. Parties engaged in them would then perceive, either that in substance they agreed together, or that their difference was one of first principles. This is the great object to be aimed at in the present state, though confessedly a very arduous one. We need not dispute, we need not prove, – we need but define. At all events, let us, if we can, do this first of all; and then see who are left for us to dispute with, what is left for us to prove. ... When men understand what each other mean, they see, for the most part, that controversy is either superfluous or hopeless.[68]

Some lecture notes he prepared in 1859 on the subject of 'Logic' reveal some interesting details of Newman's approach to philosophy.[69] On discussing the division and order followed by various authors in their teaching of philosophy he concludes: 'I begin with Logic, both because it is usual to do so, and because it has the best claim to be first considered.' It is apparent that one of his reasons for starting with logic is to be able to establish some order regarding the various systems of terminology used by philosophers. However, while criticizing Mill for confusing intellectual conception with imagination, later in these same notes he states that: 'Here we must define our word "conception" – and thus metaphysics are a sort of basis of logic.' As has already been pointed out, Newman is well aware that in philosophy there is a risk of confusing our thinking with reality. Such a danger is even greater for those who are about to commence the study of philosophy. Consequently, we might have expected him to propose metaphysics as the first subject to be considered. His decision to start with logic in the formal study of philosophy was probably purely practical, 'because it is usual to do so'. This was the order then followed in the teaching of scholastic philosophy. Alternatively, his choice may have been governed by the priority given to it by Aristotle. That is to say, to put logic first in virtue of its great instrumental usefulness in terms of studying all the other branches of philosophy.

Theory of Knowledge

In these same notes he discusses the definitions given to logic by several authors. For instance, he quotes that of Whately as, 'the art of reasoning'. He proposes his own definition: 'The Science of Proof or Inference'. He comments that this agrees with other thinkers such as Aristotle and Mill. Echoing the thought of Aristotle, he says that as an instrumental art and science, 'It is not concerned with the truth or falsehood of the subject matter, but is hypothetical. The only truth it is concerned with is that of the act of inference.' He then clarifies: 'By "inference" is meant the process of the mind to what is unknown from, besides, and because of what is known. A is true, therefore B is true.'

These notes show that Newman does not agree with the then current scholastic division of logic into formal and material. He prefers to consider formal logic as 'that instrumental science or art, to which I would confine the name of Logic'. He argues that a separate science is needed, 'which is concerned with truth and certainty'. Then he proposes what almost amounts to a definition of the 'science of knowledge', the science that deals with the relationship between reality and the operations of our intellect:

Which treats of the connection of those two with each other; of their mutual action, and intercommunion; on the one hand of the channels by which external objects are introduced into the soul, and on the other, the criteria by which we are certain that we have possession of them and distinguish them from counterfeits.[70]

He then says that the objective of this science is 'the ascertainment of truth', and calls it 'the science of knowledge ... Noology or Gnoseology'. On other occasions he uses different terminology to refer to the theory of knowledge, for example, 'Mental Philosophy', 'Philosophy of Mind', or 'mental science'.[71]

Speaking of the purpose of the *Grammar* he places it squarely within the context of 'the science of knowledge' when he affirms: 'I would confine myself to the truth of things, and the mind's certitude of that truth.'[72]

On learning of Newman's approach to reality a contemporary critical thinker might easily be tempted to label him as a naïve realist. The intuition of being is his first self-evident truth. This leads him to affirm that the intellect is able to know reality, and there is no further need for justification. He has no doubt, as both Sillem and Dessain observe, about the ability of the intellect to know reality in all its richness of being.[73] On various occasions and in different ways, he affirms:

> Now truth cannot change; what is once truth is always truth; and the human mind is made for truth, and so rests in truth, as it cannot rest in falsehood. ... the intellect, which is made for truth, can attain truth, and, having attained it, can keep it, can recognise it, and preserve the recognition.[74]

Fundamental to the theory of knowledge proposed by many contemporary philosophers is the necessity to justify, on rational grounds, the ability of the intellect to know reality. The realism of Newman does not entertain any such problem. His writings do not contain any discussion about what today is referred to as critical realism, or the critique of knowledge. The closest he seems to come to considering this question is when introducing his section on self-evident truths in the *Grammar*. He explains that, 'our trust in our powers of reasoning and memory, that is, our implicit assent to their telling truly' cannot be taken as a self-evident truth. He continues by saying that: 'We act according to our nature, by means of ourselves, when we remember or reason. We are as little able to accept or reject our mental constitution, as our being.'[75] In other words, although on some occasions our faculties do err, that is no reason for doubting our ability to know reality through our senses and intellect.

There is no place in Newman's theory of knowledge, as Jaki also observes, for what is now known as methodological doubt.[76] In his *Grammar* he severely criticizes those who advocate that, 'we have no right in philosophy to make any assumption whatever, and that we ought to begin with a universal doubt'. On the other hand, this does not exclude having a positive sense of criticism, a 'reasonable scepticism', with respect to the assumptions with which we begin our reasoning. He explains:

> That we ought to begin with believing every thing that is offered to our acceptance, than that it is our duty to doubt of everything. The former, indeed, seems the true way of learning. In that case, we soon discover and discard what is contradictory to itself; and error having always some portion of truth in it, and the truth having a reality which error has not, we may expect, that when there is an honest purpose and fair talents, we shall somehow make our way forward, the error falling off from the mind, and the truth developing and occupying it.[77]

It seems to me that such an approach to philosophy is rather reminiscent of that of Plato and Aristotle. The apparent difficulty of making progress in knowledge is not therefore taken as suggesting impossibility, but rather as posing a challenge to the intellect.

Newman is adamant in his dislike for philosophies that pursue the 'obstinate assumption that all things must be reduced to *one* principle'.[78] He says that: 'Descartes, . . . was too independent in his inquiries to be always correct in his conclusions.'[79] He seems to be well aware of the danger inherent in attempting to build a philosophy on some first principle akin to the Cartesian *cogito ergo sum*. He only gives this topic a passing consideration in his writings.[80] Philosophy begins with our acceptance of reality as we find it. He affirms that: 'Our being, with its faculties, mind and body, is a fact not admitting of question, all things being of necessity referred to it, not it to other things.'[81] His gnoseology will be dealt with in detail in the chapters that follow.

The *Grammar* and Methodology

The *Grammar* is not only the primary source for Newman's philosophy but also, more than any other of his works, illustrates his philosophical method. In order to understand better his methodology I think it is relevant to begin by considering the nature of the *Grammar*. As we have seen, he referred to it as one of his 'five constructive books'. It must also be remembered, as stated in the opening paragraph of this chapter, that he did not intend it to be a systematic treatise. For example, in answering one of his critics he says that it is not 'necessary to be exactissimus in a work which is a conversational essay, not a didactic treatise'.[82] This point is also illustrated, as noticed by Artz, by its full title, *An Essay in Aid of a Grammar of Assent*.[83] In a letter of April 1870 Newman explains that: 'I called it an Essay, as it really is, because it is an analytical inquiry – a Grammar ought to be synthetical.'[84] Ward suggests that he used the word essay 'as if to disclaim as emphatically as possible any pretension to a final treatment of his subject'.[85] One year after its publication he said in another letter: 'I am sensible it may be full of defects, and certainly characterised by incompleteness and crudeness, but it is something to have started a problem, and mapped in part of a country, if I have done nothing more.'[86]

He makes it abundantly clear in his *Grammar* that he is not proposing some hypothetical theory with regard to the science of knowledge. When dealing with the intellectual act of Assent he affirms that he is 'treating the subject then, not according to *a priori* fitness, but according to the facts of human nature, as they are found in the concrete action of life'.[87] He begins his penultimate chapter with the statement: 'My object in the foregoing pages has been, not to form a theory which may account for these phenomena of the intellect of which they treat ... but to ascertain which is the matter of fact as regards them.'[88]

As Ker remarks, although he did not consider it in any way definitive or complete, this does not imply that the *Grammar* is lacking in scientific rigour.[89] Apart from taking the form of an essay it is also a grammar, which Newman defined as: 'the scientific analysis of language'.[90] In this case, it is the grammar of the operations of the intellect leading to our acquisition of knowledge. He writes in the spirit of the explorer, who carefully traces out the path he himself has taken in order to help those who wish to come after him. Within the general context of the philosophy of religion the *Grammar* presents us with an accurate sketch of a theory of knowledge that maps out in some detail the various elements involved that lead to our knowledge of reality.

He does not make great use of philosophical terminology and formal definitions in his *Grammar*. Where he deems it necessary for the sake of clarity he does designate specific terms to some of his key concepts. In some notes that he drafted in preparation for writing this work he says: 'I do not wish to attempt definitions of the things about which I am to write, further than is practically useful towards attaining a clear and consistent idea of them.'[91] On the other hand, he appreciates the importance of terminology and definitions as a guarantee of scientific precision. In his lecture notes on logic already mentioned he comments that: 'This is not merely a question of words, for according to the definition, will be the treatise, and the subjects included in it.'[92] Although his method can be characterized as descriptive this does not mean that it is not at the same time both profound and precise.

In the *Grammar* he prefers to express his thought in rather ordinary language, without relying heavily on terminology. Therefore, it is more rewarding to read it with careful attention. At the same time, when he does introduce specific terminology it is essential to make sure that we have understood the meaning he wishes to give it. This is particularly relevant in those cases where the same, or similar terms, can be found in other philosophical contexts with possible different meanings. For example, as we shall see later, with regard to such words as Apprehension and Informal Inference.

Having considered the general nature of his *Grammar* we are now in a position to examine the methodology he uses to explain its philosophical content. Nowhere in his writings does he discuss methodology with respect to philosophy. However, in his *Grammar* at least he gives us a clue when he is about to apply his theory of knowledge to the question of religious faith, and states:

> I begin with expressing a sentiment, which is habitually in my thoughts, whenever they are turned to the subject of mental or moral science, and which I am as willing to apply here to the Evidences of Religion as it properly applies to Metaphysics or Ethics, viz, that in these provinces of inquiry egotism is true modesty.[93]

Here we have another expression of the primordial importance that he gives to the acquisition of self-evident truths and first principles, 'egotism is true modesty' because my knowledge is absolutely dependent on my acquiring such truths. They are the necessary starting points of all my reasoning. In addition, when it comes to communicating this knowledge to others, one can only speak for oneself, since these self-evident truths and first principles are not necessarily held universally.[94] Within this context he concludes: 'Therefore metaphysics is a conditional science, conditional on the truth of those starting points which commend themselves to me, and not perhaps to another.'[95] This statement does not imply any disparagement towards metaphysics as a science. He is simply alluding to the fact that our self-evident truths or first principles, which constitute the premises for our reasoning, are not always shared by all. I return to this topic in a later chapter.

His general principle that 'egotism is true modesty' determines his method when it comes to explaining his philosophical conclusions. The *Grammar* exhibits this very clearly. Based on detailed and profound descriptions, supported by examples and illustrations, he tries to lead the reader into sharing, or acquiring, his own self-evident truths and first principles. These will then form the premises for his subsequent arguments. It is the presence of these characteristics that enable us to refer to his method as descriptive. He himself seems to acknowledge this when, in a note to be included in the 1880 edition of his *Grammar*, he states: 'I will add, that a main reason for my writing this Essay on Assent, to which I am adding these last words, was, as far as I could, to describe the *organum investigandi* which I thought the true one.'[96]

Newman scholars have pointed out that his descriptive

method does not imply some form of psychologism.[97] His starting point in philosophy is always reality as perceived through our senses. He proposes explanations for the various operations of the intellect supported by evidence, usually drawn from universal experience together with his own, as the warrant for his conclusions. His approach is transparent. On encountering certain difficulties he is quite sincere and, neither has recourse to superficial *ad hominem* arguments, nor pretends that there are no questions needing an answer.

I think it is feasible, given our present knowledge of the phenomenological movement, to refer to Newman's method as descriptive phenomenology. I examine this claim in detail in my concluding chapter. The term phenomenon only appears occasionally in his writings. He does not appear to attribute any specific meaning to it apart from that used by the world of science at the time. For instance, he talks of the 'phenomena of sense' in terms of the information we perceive through our senses.[98] He also speaks of the 'phenomena of the intellect' when referring to some of its operations.[99]

It seems plausible to refer to his method as phenomenological if by this term we mean that he builds his philosophy on the foundation of an assiduous study of reality. That is to say, as revealed to us through our sense perception and augmented by what empirical science can teach us about its nature. His realism demands a careful analysis of the reality that we know. It implies searching for the causes and patterns according to which it behaves.

To associate his descriptive approach with empirical experience does not make him an empiricist. His use of certain phraseology common to the empiricism of his day is the result of it being more appropriate to express his realist position as opposed to that of idealism. Gilson confirms this conclusion when he says that: 'His insistence on the intensity proper to empirical experience and to our cognition of singulars, as contrasted with the weakness of all impressions caused on our minds by merely abstract notions, seems a heritage from British empiricism.'[100] In this respect I have already made mention of his great respect for scientists such as Bacon and Newton.

It is quite clear that Newman did not think that all human knowledge could ultimately be reduced to pure sense data. For example, in his *Idea of a University* he writes:

> It seems to me improper to call that passive sensation, or perception of things, which brutes seem to possess, by the name of Knowledge. When I speak of Knowledge, I mean something intellectual, something which grasps what it perceives through the senses; something which takes a view of things; which sees more than the senses convey; which reasons upon what it sees, and while it sees; which invests it with an idea.[101]

His view on intellectual abstraction is incompatible with any form of empiricism. José Morales notices the general agreement amongst Newman scholars, such as Cameron, Sillem, Artz and Fey, who affirm that he does not fall into any of the prejudices proper to the reductionism of classical empiricism.[102]

His empirical turn of mind is an expression of his profound appreciation of reality as both the source and the objective of all philosophical contemplation. He follows Aristotle in basing his philosophy on the experience of reality that is derived from our sense perception. Copleston says that this same empirical approach was the starting point of the philosophical thought of both Aquinas and Locke.[103]

Reality, the objective of our philosophical knowledge, is also its permanent reference point. The attitude of constantly referring back to reality enables the philosopher to avoid some of the pitfalls of idealism. We come to know the nature of the human intellect and its operations through a meticulous study of their effects as exhibited in the facts of human experience. Newman is acutely aware of the danger of idealism: of confusing our thought with reality, of losing touch with reality in the attempt to construct a philosophical system. When a philosophy loses contact with reality, which is its life-giving principle, then there is a serious risk of it becoming a lifeless man-made idealism. We can admire it for its logical beauty, but it is able to tell us very little about the reality it set out to explore. He seems to have this in mind when he writes in his *Grammar*:

Hence it is that an intellectual school will always have something of an esoteric character; for it is an assemblage of minds that think; their bond is unity of thought, and their words become a sort of *tessera*, not expressing thought, but symbolizing it.[104]

In order to avoid possible misunderstandings in this respect it is worth noticing the use Newman makes of the term metaphysics in his writings. He gives it the meaning, on several occasions, that was then current among British philosophers, rather than that originating from the thought of Aristotle. Two major trends dominated the philosophy of nineteenth-century Britain. First, there was empiricism together with the so-called common sense philosophies springing from the thought of Locke and Thomas Reid. On the other hand, there were the various forms of rationalism in which logic played an exaggerated role. This current was associated with the University of Oxford. The term metaphysics, influenced by this philosophical climate, had acquired a rather pejorative meaning. It had become associated with the different schools of idealism then present in continental Europe, especially in Germany. These were judged in Britain, rightly or wrongly, to have emanated from the thought of Descartes and based on a priori ideas. Such philosophies were frowned upon as being grounded on altogether unverifiable and gratuitous hypotheses, the stuff of dreamers, of those who liked to indulge in wishful thinking, or obtuse and aimless speculation. They were viewed as being the cause of confusion and philosophical scepticism. Sillem suggests that when Newman uses the term metaphysics to refer to such philosophies he has in mind thinkers such as Immanuel Kant (1724–1804), Johann Gottlieb Fichte (1762–1814), Friedrich Heinrich Jacobi (1743–1819), Georg Wilhelm Friedrich Hegel (1770–1831) or Friedrich Wilhelm Joseph Schelling (1775–1854).[105]

It is relatively easy to detect this pejorative meaning given to the word metaphysics in the writings of Newman. For instance, in his *Grammar*, when he appears to be criticizing a Kantian form of philosophy, he says that his 'aim is of a practical character', rather than 'falling into metaphysics'. He is clarifying that his intention is not to propose some kind of hypothetical theory, but rather of giving a coherent explanation of the facts: 'This is what the schoolmen, I believe, call treating a subject *in facto esse*, in contrast with *in fieri*.'[106] Another example occurs in his answer to an accusation against him of scepticism when he says, 'My turn of mind has never led me towards metaphysics; rather it has been logical, ethical, practical.'[107]

On the other hand, there are many occasions where he employs the term metaphysics with its classical meaning as found in the thought of Aristotle and Aquinas, and it has none of these negative connotations.[108] He had no hesitation, as mentioned earlier, in affirming that he would not 'be found in substance to disagree with St Thomas'. However, I think it was unfortunate that he never had the opportunity of coming to know in depth the metaphysics of being as proposed by Aquinas. Nevertheless, I feel that running through all his philosophy there is an implicit understanding of being as such, and of the myriad forms of the participation of being throughout reality as envisaged by Aquinas.

Having considered the foundations of Newman's realism together with his philosophical methodology we now turn our attention to his approach to the theory of knowledge. In the *Grammar* he gives priority to explaining how it is, in practice, that the intellect reaches ontological truth about reality. He does not propose a theory to fit the facts. His approach is to give an accurate philosophical description, according to the facts, on how the intellect reaches truth.

Notes

1. Cf. Dessain, 'Newman on the Theory and Practice of Knowledge', pp. 7, 9; Ker, 'Introduction', in *GA* (1985), p. xlviii.
2. Cf. Sillem, pp. 11–15, 108; Norris, pp. 16–19; Boekraad, *The Personal Conquest of Truth According to J. H. Newman*, pp. 255–7; Pailin, p. 122; Fey, pp. 76, 83, 118ff, 142.

3. Dessain, *John Henry Newman*, pp. 8–9; cf. ibid., p. 17.
4. Sillem, p. 108.
5. *US*, p. 205; cf. *PS* IV, pp. 201–2.
6. *US*, p. 231.
7. *GA*, p. 223 (346); cf. ibid., pp. 106 (160), 154 (236); 181 (277–8).
8. Sillem, p. 11.
9. *US*, pp. 205–6; cf. ibid., p. 222; *Phil N* II, pp. 87–91, 93–9; *Dev*, pp. 110–11; *TP* I, p. 117; *GA*, pp. 71–2 (103), 224 (346–7).
10. *US*, p. 349 footnote 5; cf. *TP I*, pp. 163–5.
11. *TP I*, p. 109; cf. ibid., pp. 63–4, 104, 126; *US*, pp. 256–7; *Idea*, p. 45; *Phil N* II, pp. 23–5; *GA*, p. 224 (347).
12. Cf. Boekraad, *The Personal Conquest of Truth According to J. H. Newman*, pp. 255–72.
13. *GA*, pp. 21 (20), 22 (22), 27 (30), 172 (265), 180 (277), 184 (282), 223 (344).
14. *GA*, pp. 173 (266), 184 (282).
15. *GA*, p. 27 (31).
16. *GA*, p. 13 (9).
17. *GA*, p. 184 (283).
18. *GA*, p. 182 (279).
19. *GA*, pp. 175 (268), 184 (283), 187 (288).
20. *GA*, pp. 175 (268), 181 (279), 187 (288), 223 (344).
21. *GA*, pp. 175 (269), 176 (270–1), 205 (317), 223 (345).
22. *GA*, p. 172 (265).
23. *US*, pp. 290–1; cf. *Idea*, pp. 111–13.
24. *TP* I, p. 118.
25. *GA*, p. 48 (64).
26. *GA*, p. 34 (42).
27. *GA*, p. 222 (344).
28. *GA*, p. 175 (269).
29. *GA*, p. 45 (60).
30. *Prepos*, pp. 283–4; cf. ibid., pp. 278–87, 292–3, 301–3; *Dev*, pp. 178–85, 325–6.
31. *GA*, p. 47 (62); TP I, pp. 64, 65, 71–2.
32. *TP* I, p. 18; cf. *GA*, pp. 116–17 (176).
33. *TP* I, p. 64; cf. *Phil N* II, p. 73.
34. *TP* I, p. 72.
35. *TP* I, p. 153.
36. Cf. *Phil N* II, p. 29; *US*, pp. 43–5; *TP* I, pp. 152–5; Aquinas,

Summa Theologiae II–II, q. 49, a. 5 ad 3.
37. *TP* I, p. 69.
38. *Phil N* II, p. 29.
39. *TP* I, p. 74. This is Newman's translation with added emphasis of Aristotle's *Nicomachean Ethics*, book VI, xi, 6.
40. *TP* I, p. 77.
41. *GA*, p. 47 (62); cf. *LD* XXIV, pp. 309–11, 314.
42. Cf. Aquinas, *Summa Theologiae* I, q. 5, a. 2.
43. Cf. *GA*, 47 (62–3), 180–1 (277), 182 (279–80), 195–6 (301–2); *US*, pp. 330–1, 349 footnote.
44. *Phil N* II, p. 8;
45. *Phil N* II, p. 35; cf. ibid., pp. 202–12.
46. *TP* I, p. 71; cf. ibid., p. 68; *Phil N* II, p. 15.
47. *GA*, p. 47 (63).
48. Cf. *GA*, pp. 73–8 (105–19), 84 (123–4), 251–2 (389–91), 268 (417), 270 (420).
49. Cf. Walgrave, *Newman. Le développement du dogme*, pp. 238–43, 247, 254–9, 380–1; ibid., 'L'actualité de Newman', pp. 19, 24–5; Holloway, pp. 158–9.
50. Cf. *PS* I, pp. 19–20, 24, 92–3, 153–4, 328; *PS* III, pp. 114ff; *PS* V, p. 84; *PS* VII, p. 64; *US*, pp. 348–9; *Dev*, pp. 111–12; *GA*, pp. 225–7 (349–52), 259–60 (402–3), 265–6 (412–13).
51. *GA*, p. 227 (351); cf. ibid., p. 145 (221); *Dev*, p. 111.
52. *GA*, pp. 48–9 (65).
53. *GA*, p. 49 (66).
54. *GA*, p. 50 (67).
55. *TP* I, pp. 64–5.
56. *GA*, pp. 50–1 (68).
57. *GA*, p. 51 (68–9); cf. *Phil N* II, pp. 150–2.
58. *GA*, p. 53 (71); cf. *TP* I, pp. 93–4.
59. *GA*, p. 182 (280); cf. ibid., p. 246 (382).
60. Cf. *GA*, pp. 198–9 (306–7).
61. Cf. *TP* I, pp. 156–7, 162; *Phil N* II, p. 125; *LD* XXX, p. 47; *LD* XXXI, p. 93 .
62. *TP* I, p. 93; cf. ibid., p. 45.
63. Cf. Jaki, *The Purpose of It All*, pp. 73–4.
64. Cf. *TP* I, pp. 40, 139, 156–7; *Idea*, pp. 221–2.
65. *Phil N* II, p. 24.
66. Cf. Aquinas, *Summa Theologiae* I, q. 44, a. 1; q. 65, a. 1.
67. *Idea*, pp. 221–2.
68. *US*, pp. 200–1; cf. ibid., pp. xiii–xiv; *Prepos*, pp. 277–91; *TP* I,

pp. 145–6; *GA*, p. 266 (413).
69. Cf. *TP* I, pp. 51–62.
70. *TP* I, pp. 54–5.
71. Cf. *Idea*, pp. 46, 55; *GA*, p. 248 (384); *TP* I, p. 140.
72. *GA*, p. 223 (344).
73. Cf. Sillem, p. 138; Dessain, *John Henry Newman*, pp. 8–9, 16, 153.
74. *GA*, p. 145 (221–2); cf. ibid., pp. 114 (172), 202 (311); *Idea*, pp. 45–6, 104, 113–14, 124–30, 248; *TP* I, p. 71.
75. *GA*, p. 46 (61).
76. Cf. Jaki, *Newman's Challenge*, p. 213.
77. *GA*, p. 243 (377).
78. *Phil N* II, p. 91.
79. *Idea*, p. 315.
80. Cf. *GA*, p. 187 (287) footnote 1; *Phil N* II, pp. 35–9, 71, 73, 89–91; *TP* I, pp. 63, 94.
81. *GA*, p. 224 (346).
82. *LD* XXV, p. 131.
83. Cf. Artz, 'Newman as Philosopher', p. 273.
84. *LD* XXV, p. 84.
85. Ward, vol. II, p. 262.
86. *LD* XXV, p. 280; cf. *LD* XXV, p. 131; Ward, vol. II, pp. 270–1.
87. *GA*, p. 116 (176).
88. *GA*, p. 222 (343).
89. Cf. Ker, 'Introduction', in *GA* (1985), p. v.
90. *Idea*, p. 334.
91. *TP* I, pp. 126–7.
92. *TP* I, p. 53.
93. *GA*, p. 248 (384); cf. *TP* I, pp. 48, 88.
94. Cf. *GA*, pp. 263–4 (409–10).
95. *Phil N* II, p. 89.
96. *GA*, p. 321 (499).
97. Cf. Sillem, p. 133; ibid., in *Phil N* II, p. 31 footnote 3; Boekraad, *The Personal Conquest of Truth*, pp. 255–72; Artz, 'Newman as Philosopher', p. 272.
98. *GA*, p. 47 (62); cf. *TP* I, pp. 39, 65, 67, 104, 106–7, 110–11, 136; *Idea*, p. 432; *Phil N* II, pp. 200, 208, 215–16.
99. *GA*, p. 222 (343).
100. Gilson, 'Introduction', in *GA* (1955), pp. 10–11.
101. *Idea*, pp. 112–13.
102. Cf. Morales, 'John Henry Newman y el movimiento de Oxford

(II)', p. 1116; Fey, pp. 8–9, 91, 95, 120.
103. Cf. Copleston, vol. V, p. 78; ibid., vol. VIII, p. 53.
104. *GA*, p. 201 (309).
105. Cf. Sillem, pp. 227–34; ibid., *Phil N* II, p. 89 footnote 3. Much of Newman's knowledge of philosophy in Germany came from his reading of Chalybäus.
106. *GA*, p. 222 (343).
107. *TP* I, p. 151; cf. *Phil N* II, pp. 27, 90–1.
108. Cf. *GA*, pp. 156 (239–40), 249 (385); *Idea*, pp. 25, 40, 53, 57, 67, 72, 100, 112, 222, 224; *Dev*, pp. 52, 54; *TP* I, pp. 39, 153; *Phil N* II, p. 89.

CHAPTER 3

APPREHENSION

Newman did not intend his *Grammar* either to be the definitive word on the subject, or to represent the complete picture. It comes as no surprise, therefore, to know that he invited positive criticism of his work. He suggested in a letter three possible ways of procedure: '1. that it should be analysed, and should bear analysis. 2. that the objections against it should be carefully collected. 3. that those objections should be answered.'[1] My intention in the following four chapters is to follow his own criteria in an appraisal of his theory of knowledge as found in the *Grammar*.

However, before launching out, I think it is worthwhile recalling my intended methodology. I stated in the introductory chapter that I would be using the fundamental concepts of the philosophy of Aquinas as a frame of reference. This should facilitate the understanding of the lesser known concepts of Newman when viewed within the framework of the more familiar ones of Aquinas. At the same time, as I have already stressed, I will take great care not to distort either the thought of Newman, or that of Aquinas. I have no intention to make false claims with regard to the views either of the one or the other.

I follow the same order in my analysis of his approach to knowledge as Newman himself in his *Grammar*. Apart from being the obvious way to do justice to his thought it also makes it easier for the reader to refer directly to the text if he so wishes. At the same time I will introduce the material found in his other writings relevant to the topic under discussion.

Those accustomed to the literary style found in his other writings may be a little surprised by the way in which he commences his *Grammar*. The title of his first chapter would not be out of place in a manual of logic: '*Modes of Holding and Apprehending Propositions*.'[2] Then, without further ado, he plunges into a linguistic analysis that almost reminds us of Aristotle's *Organon*. Language, as the reflection of human thought, takes the form of propositions that can be classified into three types: the interrogative, the conditional and the categorical proposition. These external expressions correspond to the internal mental acts of doubt, inference and assent. He then states that he will be dealing with 'propositions only in their bearing upon concrete matter, and I am mainly concerned with Assent; with Inference, in its relation to Assent, and only such inference as is not demonstration; with Doubt, hardly at all'.[3]

Those familiar with the thought of Aristotle will recognize the term 'simple apprehension' as referring to what he considered to be the first operation of the intellect. That is to say, the natural and spontaneous ability of the intellect to form concepts in the mind on coming into contact with reality perceived through our senses. These concepts relate to the essences found in the myriad beings that constitute reality. They are the intelligible forms that are abstracted, separated, from the incidental and material individuality of the reality. They are distinct from the products of our sense experience through which they were derived, but remain related to it. Simple apprehension is the way the intellect knows the essences of the beings of reality through sense experience. Newman was familiar with both the terminology and notion of simple apprehension as proposed by Aristotle.[4]

In his *Idea of a University* he portrays simple apprehension and the other operations of the intellect in the following terms:

> One of the first acts of the human mind is to take hold of and appropriate what meets the senses, and herein lies a chief distinction between man's and a brute's use of them. Brutes gaze on sights, they are arrested by sounds; and what they see and what they hear are mainly sights and sounds only. The intellect of man, on the contrary, energizes as well as his eye

or ear, and perceives in sights and sounds something beyond them. It seizes and unites what the senses present to it; it grasps and forms what need not have been seen or heard except in its constituent parts. It discerns in lines and colours, or in tones, what is beautiful and what is not. It gives them a meaning, and invests them with an idea. It gathers up a succession of notes into the expression of a whole, and calls it a melody; it has a keen sensibility towards angles and curves, lights and shadows, tints and contours. It distinguishes between rule and exception, between accident and design. It assigns phenomena to a general law, qualities to a subject, acts to a principle, and effects to a cause. In a word, it philosophizes; for I suppose Science and Philosophy, in their elementary idea, are nothing else but this habit of *viewing*, as it may be called, the objects which sense conveys to the mind, of throwing them into system, and uniting and stamping them with one form.[5]

There is a general consistency in his *Grammar* of the use of terms to denote the products of the intellect and the senses. The words, 'notion', 'concept' or 'idea' refer to the intellect. The most common terms he uses, apart from the obvious ones, with respect to the senses, external or internal, are 'informations', 'phenomena', 'sensible objects', 'perception', 'experience' and 'images'.[6] With the word 'experience' he also implies our self-knowledge: 'by experience I mean in the first instance, the results of our consciousness and of our use of our senses. By our self-consciousness we know about ourselves; by the use of our senses we are informed of things independent of us.'[7] It is important to notice that his use of the term 'image' includes, not only the products of our external senses, but also those associated with our memory, imagination and mental states.[8]

Observing that Newman gives a wider semantic range to the term 'Apprehension' in his *Grammar* than that given to it by Aristotle can help avoid possible misunderstanding. For instance, he begins by employing it both with respect to 'propositions' and their 'terms': 'By our apprehension of propositions I mean our imposition of a sense on the terms of which they are composed',[9] 'the interpretation of the terms of which it is composed',[10] 'an intelligent acceptance of the idea or of the fact which a proposition enunciates'.[11] However, later in his explanation, he uses it more in the sense of simple apprehension as understood by Aristotle.

Real and Notional Apprehension

After introducing his view on the Apprehension of propositions he proposes a distinction that, as Benard notes, assumes paramount importance in the understanding of his thought.[12] The Apprehension of a proposition can take place in two different ways. It may refer more directly to the specific realities signified by the terms of the proposition. 'Real Apprehension' is the term he uses to designate such cases. On the other hand, the content of the Apprehension may refer more directly to logical entities in the mind, endowed with some meaning and capable of being used as terms in our thinking. This is what he calls 'Notional Apprehension'. As an example he cites the proposition: 'Man is an animal.' The Apprehension of this proposition is Notional since both subject and predicate represent intellectual abstractions from individuals. Conversely, the Apprehension of the proposition, 'Philip was the father of Alexander', implies 'Real Apprehension'.[13]

What elicits Real Apprehension in one mind may only give rise to Notional Apprehension in another. This will depend, for example, on whether or not the person has had actual sense experience of the realities signified by the terms. In this case, it will give a certain ontological value to the Apprehension. The concepts resulting from such Apprehension will have an ontological dimension while at the same time being logical entities. This ontological value of concepts can vary from one mind to another. Therefore, the Apprehension of the same proposition by one person may be different from that of another. That is to say, in one mind the terms of a particular proposition may be held with Real Apprehension while in another they may only imply Notional Apprehension.

He also affirms that, since Real Apprehension implies sense perception of the realities signified in the terms, it can have a greater affect on us as humans. There is a greater likelihood that Real Apprehension will provoke some kind of human response. He emphasizes this idea in the *Grammar* on several occasions.[14]

When he first describes Apprehension in the *Grammar* he tends to stress its subjective aspects as referring to the meaning evoked in the mind by the terms of a given proposition. Real Apprehension or Notional Apprehension, as the case may be, is in the mind of the person who is the subject of the Apprehension. However, as he elaborates on his explanation, he places more importance on the objective relationship between the terms of the proposition and the realities to which they refer as determining factors in their Apprehension:

> Such are the two modes of apprehension. The terms of a proposition do or do not stand for things. If they do, then they are singular terms, for all things that are, are units. But if they do not stand for things they must stand for notions, and are common terms. Singular nouns come from experience, common from abstraction. The apprehension of the former I call real, and of the latter notional.[15]

That is to say, he now views Apprehension more in terms of the subject's appreciation of the reality signified by the terms. M. Jamie Ferreira seems to suggest that this represents a lack of coherence in his argument.[16] I think that it is simply the result of a gradual development and deepening in his explanation of the concept. He wishes to stress that Apprehension, although belonging to the mind of an individual, always has its origin in reality itself and how it was apprehended: 'What is concrete exerts a force and makes an impression on the mind which nothing abstract can rival. That is, ... because the object is more powerful, therefore so is the apprehension of it.'[17]

Real or Notional Apprehension depend on our greater or lesser Apprehension of the realities that the different terms of a proposition signify. Real Apprehension implies that we have sense experience, present or past, through our memory, of the realities associated with the terms. On the other hand, Notional Apprehension is more the result of the intellect's power of abstraction producing universal concepts that are no longer necessarily indicative of any individual reality.

In another description of this distinction he states:

> Here then we have two modes of thought, both using the same words, both having one origin, yet with nothing in common in their results. The informations of sense and sensation are the initial basis of both of them; but in the one we take hold of objects from within them, and in the other we view them outside of them; we perpetuate them as images in the one case, we transform them into notions in the other.[18]

According to his realism it is our sense perception of reality that, in the final analysis, is the source of all concepts. Real Apprehension implies a realization of the individuality of the realities signified by our concepts. This is the result of both the operation of the intellect and sense experience working in harmony. As already mentioned, this experience may be derived from both our external senses as well as the internal ones, such as memory and imagination. It may also include the experience originating from our self-consciousness: 'The apprehension which we have of our past mental acts of any kind, of hope, inquiry, effort, triumph, disappointment, suspicion, hatred, and a hundred others, is an apprehension of the memory of those definite acts, and therefore an apprehension of things.'[19]

However, it is possible to use our concepts as logical terms in our thinking without thereby implying any specific reference to individual beings present in reality. This is the case with Notional Apprehension where the emphasis is placed on concepts as logical entities. Our concepts based on Real Apprehension will have greater ontological comprehension, while those of Notional Apprehension will exhibit greater logical extension. He explains:

To apprehend notionally is to have breadth of mind, but to be shallow, to apprehend really is to be deep, but to be narrow-minded. The latter is the conservative principle of knowledge, and the former the principle of its advancement. Without the apprehension of notions we should forever pace round one small circle of knowledge; without a firm hold upon things, we shall waste ourselves in vague speculations.[20]

Concepts, by their very nature, originate from our sense experience and consequently have, to a greater or lesser extent, both ontological and logical aspects in the mind. Thus, in practice, these two ways of viewing Apprehension are mutually complementary and each 'has its own excellence and serviceableness, and each has its own imperfection'.

It is worth noting that Newman's distinction does not imply a radical division into two mutually exclusive categories. The distinction between Real and Notional Apprehension is based on whether the resulting concepts have a more or less profound ontological depth. Therefore it is clear that it is one of degree. Real Apprehension is that Apprehension where the concepts, derived from personal experience, are related to a greater extent to an individual being, or beings, in reality. On the other hand, Notional Apprehension implies that, although originating in some way from sense experience, the ontological depth of the concepts is only sufficient for their use as mental terms in a logical discourse. All concepts, by their very nature, have both an ontological and logical dimension. They all have some ontological relationship, however minimal, since their source is reality as apprehended by the intellect viewed through our senses. At the same time, all concepts are logical entities, and can be used as such in our reasoning. Thus, it is a distinction that is open to degrees of more or less: 'Our apprehension of a proposition varies in strength, and that it is stronger when it is concerned with a proposition expressive of things than when concerned with a proposition expressive of notions.'

Apprehension is a function both of sense perception and intellectual abstraction. The realist will tend to place the emphasis on the ontological aspects rather than the logical, hence he will give priority to Real Apprehension. Newman explains:

> However, real apprehension has the precedence, as being the scope and end and the test of notional; and the fuller is the mind's hold upon things or what it considers such, the more fertile is it in its aspect of them, and the more practical in its definitions.[21]

His division of Apprehension into Real and Notional rather suggests that he appreciated the classical mental distinction between the metaphysical universal and the logical universal. The same universal concept can be considered from two different points of view. On the one hand, it can be viewed in itself according to its real and ontological content in terms of its relationship to the reality it signifies. Alternatively, this same concept can be viewed with respect to its very universality, as signifying an essence of a real being, but in terms of it being a concept in the mind. In other words, the focus is on the logical properties that this concept possesses. The first of these two cases is that of the metaphysical universal, while the latter is referred to as a logical universal. The consideration of the metaphysical properties of the universal focuses on its comprehension. Alternatively, viewing the universal in terms of its logical aspects concentrates on its extension and universal predication.

The way that Newman describes these two forms of Apprehension suggests that the distinction between Real and Notional can only be made after a reflective analysis of the content of the Apprehension. However, if Apprehension is understood in the basic Aristotelian sense which I believe is Newman's intention, then it is worth noticing that in itself it is an operation of the intellect which is not reflective. It is a direct consequence of the contact with reality of the intellect through sense experience. This of course does not prevent it from being subsequently analysed in order to classify it as Real or Notional.

Empiricism

There is an inherent danger in attempting to oversimplify his distinction between Real and Notional Apprehension. The failure to appreciate that Apprehension always includes both ontological and logical elements to some degree may lead to false interpretations. I believe this to be the case with Thomas J. Norris who describes this distinction as being: 'between "things-to-us" categories and "things-between-themselves" categories. The former are experimental, personal and therefore self-involving categories, while the latter are explanatory, scientific and non-involving categories.'[22] Such an interpretation, without further explanation, risks draining Newman's concept of Apprehension of its ontological content, and reducing it to some form of empirical classification. He gives great importance to the role of sense experience with respect to Real Apprehension, but this does not make him an empiricist. He is not implying that knowledge remains at the level of the information gathered by our external senses together with that stored in the memory, or conjured up by the imagination. At the same time, with respect to Notional Apprehension, an interpretation of this kind can lead to understanding it as just the result of observing generalizations, similarities and differences, amongst the multitude of the individual beings that come under the scrutiny of our senses. In other words, it is reduced to some kind of nominalist category. Newman was well aware of the metaphysical emptiness of both empiricism and nominalism.

As we have seen, he took an interest in Mill's *System of Logic, Ratiocinative and Inductive* that was then becoming fashionable in the world of science. In 1857 he made some comments on this work. Noticing what he understands to be Mill's tendency towards empiricism, he exclaims 'but, metaphysically, it seems dangerous to lay no stress on the active power of the mind, and to appear to resolve all phenomena into passive sensations'.[23] In the same gloss he refers to something he wrote on the role of the intellect in relation to the senses where he describes this 'active power of the mind'. This eventually appeared in his *Idea of a University*. I have already quoted this text in connection with his understanding of simple apprehension.[24] The distinction that he makes between the role of the senses and that of the intellect shows clearly that he is no empiricist. Another example is found in his *Idea of a University* where he remarks:

> Without pretending to metaphysical exactness of phraseology, which would be unsuitable to an occasion like this, I say, it seems to me improper to call that passive sensation or perception of things which brutes seem to possess by the name of knowledge. When I speak of knowledge, I mean something intellectual, something which grasps what it perceives through the senses; something which takes a view of things; which sees more than the senses convey; which reasons upon what it sees, and while it sees; which invests it with an idea. It expresses itself, not in a mere enunciation, but by an enthymeme: it is of the nature of science from the first, and in this consists its dignity.[25]

Newman's view of intellectual abstraction, as understood in the Aristotelian sense, also shows that he is no empiricist. In his already quoted lecture notes on logic he says: 'Again the word ratio includes powers quite distinct from each other; viz the power of abstraction and the possession of first principles, one of which surely is a process, but the other a habit.'[26] He returns in these notes to refer to abstraction: 'Surely the faculty which I speak of is the power of taking views or aspects. Mill will say that it is attending to one part of a fact – but it is more than this – there is an act of mental separation.'[27] In another set of notes he even designates the term 'regard' to the intellect's active ability of abstraction.[28] His *Philosophical Notebook* includes an entry where he says that abstraction does not 'imply generalization or comparison' as Mill had proposed, but that the intellect is able to abstract concepts from our sense observation of 'but one horse or dog', of one individual being.[29] It is apparent that his understanding of abstraction follows that of Aristotle and is not compatible with the kind of empiricism associated with Mill.

Newman distinguishes between the concepts derived from intellectual abstraction through sense perception, and the sense experience itself, including what is contained in our memory or modified by our imagination. In another gloss on Mill's *Logic* he is critical of what he deems to be his lack of clarity on this point: 'Does he not confuse conception with imagination? ... but there are many things which we conceive, or (whatever word we use) which we hold before our intellect, which we cannot imagine. Abstract words imply conceptions which are not still imaginations.'[30] He returns to this topic in later notes of the same year:

> Imagination is distinct from reason, but mistaken for it. What is *strange*, is to the imagination *false*. It tends to doubt whatever is strange. Experience is the measure of truth to imagination ... Since man is a being of limited (powers and) knowledge, the conclusions which reason arrives at are necessarily strange, and therefore to the imagination untrue.[31]

In his *Grammar* he criticizes 'the school of Hume' that tended to confuse the products of imagination with the conclusions of reason when considering the general universal order found in nature:

> Their imagination usurps the functions of reason; and they cannot bring themselves even to entertain as a hypothesis (and this is all that they are asked to do) a thought contrary to that vivid impression of which they are the victims, that the uniformity of nature, which they witness hour by hour, is equivalent to a necessary, inviolable law.[32]

The distinction between reason and imagination is a recurrent theme in his writings.[33] This provides further evidence that he was no empiricist.

I also think that Copleston's appraisal of Real and Notional Apprehension, not unlike that of Norris, is prone to an empiricist interpretation when he wrote: 'But the general thesis seems to be reasonably clear. Apprehension or understanding of a term which stands for a thing or person is called real, while apprehension of an abstract idea or universal concept is called notional.'[34] Such a simplification seems to blur the fact that both the metaphysical and logical orders coexist in the mind and cannot be separated in such a radical way. Furthermore, his use of the word 'understanding' with regard to Apprehension is also confusing since it suggests an intellectual act that is already reflective. Newman explains:

> I have used the word *apprehension* and not *understanding*, because the latter word is of uncertain meaning, standing sometimes for the faculty or act of conceiving a proposition, sometimes for that of comprehending it, neither of which come into the sense of *apprehension*.[35]

We may have Apprehension of the individual terms of a proposition without necessarily understanding the meaning of it as a whole, which may need a reflective act of the intellect.

Universals

As in the case of empiricism it is also relevant to clarify Newman's position in the case of universal concepts since he has also been accused of both conceptualism and nominalism. To introduce this topic I quote from a letter, written soon after the publication of the *Grammar*, in which he replies to one of his critics:

> As for the writer who says that *the book* does not follow the scholastic system, I say What is the scholastic *system*? I never heard of it. The ultra-realism of the writer who considers the *ideas* as separate *entities* was not held by *all* the scholastics nor is it held by the modern Catholic metaphysicians.[36]

The critic in question was Charles Meynell, one of the leading experts of scholasticism at the time, whom he had asked to give his opinion on the *Grammar* before its publication. It can be seen from this statement that Newman did not consider universals, as such, to have any existence as individual beings.

He presents this subject in his lecture notes on logic in the following way:

It will be said that ideas and things go together, and therefore the question is unimportant – but there is the case in which there is, or is imagined, an idea without a thing, that is, the case of Universals – Accordingly those then on the side of Things against Ideas, say that there are *not* universal ideas; and a controversy ensues which is nothing else than a portion of the old scholastic controversy, between the Nominalists, Realists, and Conceptionalists.[37]

He continues by stating his own view as a realist:

'To take the part of Ideas against Things'. My own long habit has been the same – and it is difficult for me for that reason to do otherwise, but I confess the onus probandi is with those who maintain Universals, and it is difficult to prove their necessity – and taking that question away, it certainly does seem more simple and natural to say the words stand for the things.[38]

Unfortunately, while admitting this 'onus probandi', he is not forthcoming with an explanation.

The same view is expressed in his *Grammar*, that the universal concept does not have any independent being as such, in its own right. Reality consists of individual beings:

All things in the exterior world are unit and individual, and are nothing else; but the mind not only contemplates those unit realities, as they exist, but has the gift, by an act of creation, of bringing before it abstractions and generalizations, which have no existence, no counterpart, out of it.[39]

Later on he returns to the same idea: 'Let units come first, and (so-called) universals second; let universals minister to units, not units be sacrificed to universals.'[40] He then comes to the conclusion:

> Nor does any real thing admit, by any calculus of logic, of being dissected into all the possible general notions which it admits, nor, in consequence, of being recomposed out of them; though the attempt thus to treat it is more unpromising in proportion to the intricacy and completeness of its make. ... We recognise and appropriate aspects of them, a logic is useful to us in registering these aspects and what they imply; but it does not give us to know even one individual being.[41]

At the same time he is well aware that the universal concept is not only a being of reason, a logical entity, but signifies a real essence, quiddity, as subsisting in particular beings. Although the universal concept does not correspond to an individual being, as such, it does have a specific relationship to reality. Referring to the nature of universals in some papers of 1868, drafted in preparation for writing his *Grammar*, he introduces this topic stating that, while he is 'little versed in the controversy', the answer he is about to give he has held 'these forty years strenuously'. He continues with the consideration of several examples of universal concepts, and then affirms 'we have a sense of these as realities'; that they are the 'mode of apprehending a quality'; and that 'it has its *root* in that which is a thing'.[42] His commentary remains at the level of describing the facts of our experience without offering any metaphysical explanation.

In the *Grammar*, when discussing self-evident truths as universal concepts, he refers to their relationship with reality in the following terms: 'Such notions indeed are an evidence of the reality of the special sentiments in particular instances, without which they would not have been formed; but in themselves they are abstractions from facts, not elementary truths prior to reasoning.'[43]

A universal concept can be predicated of an individual being, while at the same time retaining its meaning as referring to the same essence in many beings. The universality of concepts is based on the participation of beings in certain perfections that are common to all of them. The ultimate subject of the universal is the individual subsistent being which is what exists in reality. Our concepts, as the result of intellectual abstraction, form an integral part of the cognitive process and are the proper object of our intellect as such. However, the ultimate objective of the intellect is to know reality as it is. This is achieved through the intellectual act of judgement or assent, when it affirms that a certain concept can correctly be predicated of a certain being in reality.

Newman has been criticized for his view on universals. Benard accused him of being a conceptualist.[44] Bearing in mind what we have just seen such an opinion is untenable. They are 'not elementary truths prior to reasoning'. Martin C. D'Arcy, on the other hand, after referring to the *Grammar* as 'the master-piece which no one can neglect', concludes that Newman proposes 'what is no better than a nominalist theory of knowledge'.[45] This accusation is likewise incompatible with Newman's view of universals as the result of intellectual abstraction from sense experience, and that they do express aspects of reality found in individual beings.

Jaki has also considered Newman's thinking on this topic pointing out the importance of understanding universals correctly in order to elaborate a coherent philosophy. In the first instance he gives a positive appraisal affirming that 'Newman holds high universal truth throughout the *Grammar*' and that, 'without having studied Thomas' doctrines on universals and the analogy of being, Newman almost articulates them'.[46] He then refers us to a place in the *Grammar* where, talking of the universal concept 'man', Newman says that 'he is made the logarithm of his true self, and in that shape is worked with the ease and satisfaction of logarithms'.[47] Jaki comments that with this statement 'Neothomists ... were dealt a great injustice', and continues by saying that this 'remark is a descriptive marvel and a philosophical near disaster'.[48] It is difficult to understand why Jaki introduces 'neothomists' in the context of the *Grammar*.

Newman was not a neo-thomist, nor was he writing for the benefit of neo-thomists. As we have seen, his approach is descriptive with respect to the facts rather than that of proposing metaphysical theories about them. For example, referring to the fact that we experience the phenomena of certitude, he comments: 'This is what the schoolmen, I believe, call treating a subject *in facto esse*, in contrast with *in fieri*. Had I attempted the latter, I should have been falling into metaphysics; but my aim is of a practical character.'[49] I feel that it is quite unfair to criticize Newman for not entering into metaphysical explanations when he openly declares that this was not his intention in the *Grammar*.

On the other hand, it is easy to appreciate Jaki's conclusion about Newman's remark being 'A descriptive marvel' on considering the mathematical metaphor that he applies to this concept. Just as in arithmetic, with the help of logarithms the laborious multiplication or division is reduced to simple addition or subtraction, so in logic the concept 'man' can be manipulated with ease in any dialectic exercise. However, I cannot agree with Jaki's assessment about it being 'a philosophical near disaster'. Even Newman calls his metaphor 'harsh', which would suggest that he is deliberately exaggerating for the sake of effect. His affirmation can surely be understood in the context of the concept 'man' being considered as a logical universal, as opposed to a metaphysical universal, according to the distinction already mentioned. The concept 'man', derived through total abstraction from the apprehension of individuals, is an example of a concrete concept. In other words, it principally signifies the universal nature of the being, but potentially it also expresses the individual subject having that nature. When viewed as a logical universal the focus is on its extension rather than its comprehension. That is to say, in this case Newman is thinking of the universal predicability of this concept.

Furthermore, in considering the concept 'man' as a logical universal, he is not thereby denying that this same concept can also be viewed as a metaphysical universal, referring to the nature of every individual man. For example, as in its meaning in the proposition: man is mortal. He is only affirming, albeit in an exaggerated way, that universal predicability is a property which universals possess only insofar as they are found in the mind. This would seem to be confirmed when Newman concludes, several paragraphs later, that: 'We fancy that we are doing justice to individual man and things by making them a mere *synthesis* of qualities, as if any number whatever of abstractions would, by being fused together, be equivalent to one concrete.'[50] The obvious implication of this statement is that he is asserting the priority of the metaphysical universal over the logical universal. The fact that he views Real and Notional Apprehension as complementary implies that he also appreciates the complementary value of the metaphysical universal and logical universal.

It is interesting to note that Gilson, while explaining the teaching of Aquinas on universals, also agrees with Newman on this point when he concludes:

> Reality is not made up of abstract notions ordered according to some pattern as if they were so many fragments of a mental mosaic. The abstract apprehension and coordination of essences is an absolutely necessary moment in the intellectual activity of man, but it is not the supreme achievement of the human intellect; for the ultimate end of the intellect is to conceive reality such as it is, and reality simply is not a mosaic of essences.[51]

Together with the evidence just presented, and considering the general tenor of his writings, I find nothing to suggest any serious inconsistency in Newman's view of universals with that of Aquinas.[52]

It seems to me that his distinction between Real and Notional Apprehension also shows Newman's awareness of the danger of idealism in its tendency to confuse thinking with knowing. This distinction draws our attention to the fact that our thoughts simultaneously imply both ontological and logical relationships. They have certain relationships to the beings of reality. However, at the same time, they possess logical relationships among themselves in the mind. If these two orders, the meta-physical and logical, are not carefully distinguished then it can lead to confusion, or error, regarding our knowledge of reality. It is the ontological dimension of our concepts that must take precedence since this is the origin of, and that which gives rise to, the logical order. The beings of reality constitute the source for our beings of reason, our thought.

Concluding my analysis of Newman's view of Apprehension I would like to reiterate three aspects that should be especially borne in mind in relation to his theory of knowledge. Firstly, he understands the intellectual act of Apprehension in a very general way. It can refer to the meaning elicited in our minds by a proposition and its terms, or it can imply our concepts as the result of intellectual abstraction from our sense experience of the myriad beings which make up reality. Secondly, although ultimately related to the objective reality given in our sense experience together with our intellectual abstraction of the same reality, Apprehension is personal. Therefore it can vary in quality from person to person especially with respect to Real Apprehension. And finally, because of this variation according to personal experience, the distinction can be made between Real Apprehension and Notional Apprehension which is one of degree, since all Apprehension involves both ontological and logical aspects.

Notes

1. *LD* XXV, p. 152.
2. *GA*, p. 9 (3).
3. *GA*, pp. 11–12 (7).
4. Cf. *Phil N* II, p. 71.
5. *Idea*, pp. 74–5; cf. *US*, pp. 205–7.
6. Cf. *GA*, pp. 12 (9), 23 (25), 24–5 (26–7), 25 (28), 26 (29), 27 (30), 29 (34), 46 (62), 47 (62), 60 (83), *passim*.
7. *TP* I, p. 109.
8. Cf. *TP* I, pp. 137–8.
9. *GA*, p. 12 (9).
10. *GA*, p. 16 (13).

11. *GA*, p. 20 (20).
12. Cf. Benard, p. 160.
13. *GA*, p. 13 (9–10); cf. ibid., p. 20 (19).
14. Cf. *GA*, pp. 14 (12), 31 (36), 32 (37–8).
15. *GA*, p. 22 (22–3).
16. Ferreira, p. 20.
17. *GA*, p. 31 (36).
18. *GA*, p. 29 (34).
19. *GA*, p. 24 (25).
20. *GA*, p. 29 (34), cf. ibid., pp. 47 (62), 48 (63); *TP* I, p. 60.
21. *GA*, p. 30 (34).
22. Norris, p. 190; cf. ibid., pp. 30, 32, 35, 187, 205.
23. *TP* I, p. 39.
24. Cf. pp. 48–9 above. In the gloss Newman makes reference to his *Discourses on the Scope and Nature of University Education* (Dublin, 1852), p. 107. These subsequently became the first part of his *The Idea of a University Defined and Illustrated* and the text quoted is in *Idea*, pp. 74–5.
25. *Idea*, pp. 112–13.
26. *TP* I, p. 52; cf. *GA*, pp. 22 (23), 60 (83).
27. *TP* I, p. 59.
28. *TP* I, p. 63.
29. *Phil N* II, p. 13, cf. ibid., pp. 9–21.
30. *TP* I, p. 41.
31. *TP* I, p. 47.
32. *GA*, p. 58 (81).
33. Cf. *US*, p. 9; *Phil N* II, pp. 152, 155, 202; *TP* I, pp. 93–4, 112–19, 136–7.
34. Copleston, vol. VIII, p. 517.
35. *GA*, p. 20 (19).
36. *LD* XXV, p. 79.
37. *TP* I, p. 56.
38. *TP* I, p. 56.
39. *GA*, pp. 12–13 (9).
40. *GA*, p. 182 (279).
41. *GA*, p. 184 (282–3).
42. *TP* I, pp. 135–6.
43. *GA*, p. 49 (65); cf. ibid., pp. 47 (62), 170 (261).
44. Cf. Benard, pp. 195–6.
45. Cf. D'Arcy, pp. 107, 148.
46. Jaki, *Newman's Challenge*, p. 210.

47. *GA*, p. 27 (31).
48. Jaki, *Newman's Challenge*, p. 211.
49. *GA*, p. 222 (344).
50. *GA*, p. 29 (33).
51. Gilson, *Elements of Christian Philosophy*, p. 251; cf. Aquinas, *In I Sent.*, d. 19, q. 5, a. 1.
52. Cf. Aquinas, *Summa Theologiae* I, q. 85, a. 3.

CHAPTER 4

ASSENT

As its title proclaims the *Grammar* is 'mainly concerned with Assent'.[1] It forms the central core of the book and everything else is linked to it. Newman's first chapter, *Modes of Holding and Apprehending Propositions*, contains definite echoes of the traditional Aristotelian division of the operations of the intellect into simple apprehension, judgement and reasoning. He introduces this topic with a consideration of the division of propositions into the 'interrogative', 'conditional' and 'categorical' form. These correspond to the three mental acts of 'Doubt, Inference, and Assent. A question is the expression of a doubt; a conclusion is the expression of an act of inference, and an assertion is the expression of an act of assent.'[2] The three forms of the proposition, whether they correspond to mental acts or to the external enunciation of them, are clearly distinguishable. Doubt, expressed in the form of a question, implies a lack of knowledge. The conclusion of an inference, or rational discourse, is conditional in so far as its veracity depends on that of the propositions which constitute the inference. On the other hand the assertion, or categorical proposition, is the counterpart of the intellectual act of judgement or Assent to this proposition as true. The act of Assent is given unconditionally otherwise it cannot be 'represented by assertion'. The unconditional or unreserved nature of our act of Assent is one of its essential properties. This property of the mind's Assent to propositions is one of Newman's key concepts in the understanding of his theory of knowledge.

Later in this chapter I will consider it in detail.

It is by Assent that we acquire and advance in knowledge. This is the operation of the intellect by which we personally affirm as true that which is expressed in an enunciated proposition or a mental assertion. In some notes of about 1860 in which Newman gives some short descriptive definitions, he affirms:

> *True and false*, is applied to thoughts, and denotes the exact agreement or disagreement of thought with the thing to which it belongs.
> *An assent of the mind*. An assent is thought. To assent is to decide this thought is a thing, or this thought is true. If this is so, really, it is a right assent; if not so, it is a wrong assent.[3]

These statements suggest that Newman is in agreement with the classical definition of ontological truth as expressed in the tradition of Aquinas, namely, the adequation of intellect and thing (*adequatio intellectus et rei*); the agreement of the concept with the reality in question.[4] Truth is given in the Assent to a mental assertion when its meaning does in fact correspond to reality: 'the object of Assent is a truth'.[5] In other words, we come to know reality through our Assents. In the *Grammar* he affirms:

> Let the proposition to which the assent is given be as absolutely true as the reflex act pronounces it to be, that is, objectively true as well as subjectively, then the assent may be called a *perception*, the conviction a *certitude*, the proposition of truth a *certainty*, or thing known, or a matter of *knowledge*, and to assent to it is to *know*.[6]

In order to avoid confusion it is worth noticing that his use here of the word perception refers to the product of the intellect, rather than its usual reference in the *Grammar* to our sense experience.

The second chapter of the Grammar is entitled *Assent Considered as Apprehensive*. It deals with the intellectual apprehension of the terms of a proposition necessary for the intellect to be able to Assent to it. For instance, to be able to Assent to the proposition that: x is y, demands at least some apprehension of the predicate y. Something must be apprehended of the term y if it is to be predicated of x. In this way it is possible for the intellect to Assent to the proposition: x is y. That is to say, the possibility of giving Assent to a proposition is conditional on there being at least some Apprehension of the terms of the predicate. Assent may also be given to a proposition in an indirect way. This is the case where the mind considers such a proposition to be the subject of an extended proposition such as: x is y, is true. In this case it is possible to apprehend the predicate: is true, and so Assent can be given to the complete proposition. In other words, Assent is given indirectly to the proposition that constitutes its subject. At this stage Newman only deals with the act of Assent in itself without considering the possible circumstances under which the intellect might posit such an Assent. However, he discusses the case of Assent given as a consequence of the assertion of another person. For example, to a proposition such as: 'My mother's word, that x is y, 'is the truth.' The authority of another person may provide the grounds and justification for such an Assent. In this case our Apprehension includes that relationship of faith and trust in the word of another. He affirms that, although there are these different ways of considering an Assent, the Assent itself always remains an unconditional act of the intellect.

At the same time, each Assent may have a different effectiveness in the person making it as regards eliciting further human acts. For instance, an Assent based on the veracity of another assumes something of the value of the relationship of the person making the Assent with the other. While Assent as such is always unconditional it does tend to take on something of the character of the Apprehension on which it is based. Although the act of Assent is complete in itself, its effects, in terms of possible future human actions by its subject, can be related to the concomitant Apprehension which accompanied it.

Newman's choice to employ the term Assent in the *Grammar*, as opposed to the more traditional one of judgement, to refer to this operation of the intellect would appear to be quite deliberate. It appears in his philosophy as early as 1853 when he writes in private notes: '*Assent* is the acceptance of a proposition as true.'[7] In his writings there is no explanation of his preference for this term. I think the most obvious reason is that he wished to avoid the possible risk of confusing the Assent of the intellect with its consequent external enunciation as a proposition. In classical logic such a proposition is usually referred to as a judgement. Using the term Assent is more suggestive of it being a personal act of the intellect which is what he wishes to stress:

> Assent I have described to be a mental assertion; in its very nature then it is of the mind, and not of the lips. We can assert without assenting; assent is more than assertion just by this much, that it is accompanied by some apprehension of the matter asserted.[8]

The word Assent, rather than judgement, is more suggestive of the role of the will and the moral factors which affect our human acts. It can be seen as his attempt to dissociate himself from the rather stereotyped associations that the term judgement had acquired in the propositional logic of his day. The act of Assent involves the whole person directed by the intellect and commanded by the will. On the other hand, the expressed proposition of this Assent, or of the reasoning process that possibly led to it, is quite distinct from the mental act of Assent. This preference for the term Assent can be seen as one more aspect of Newman's constant affirmation of the unity of man in all his actions.

Given the relationship between Apprehension and Assent it comes as no surprise to find that in his *Grammar* he also distinguishes between 'Notional' and 'Real Assent'. As with Apprehension this distinction is one of degree and simply represents the different antecedent or concomitant conditions under which the Assent is made. Accordingly, he designates as Real Assent that assent which is preceded and accompanied with Real Apprehension. On the other hand, Notional Assent is its counterpart with respect to Notional Apprehension. In either case he affirms that Assent is always an unconditional act of the intellect. However, with respect to whether a particular Assent will have any influence on future human acts depends usually on the nature of the Apprehension involved. Accordingly, Real Assent may spark off a response in terms of further human acts more readily than a Notional Assent.[9]

Since Newman considers this distinction to be so important in his approach to knowledge it is worth recalling the basis on which he differentiates between Real and Notional. The intellectual Apprehension that involves a more profound perception of the reality in all its ontological richness, as signified by the terms of a proposition, is designated as Real. If subsequently Assent is given to such a proposition where there has been Real Apprehension then this is referred to as a Real Assent. Similarly, the Assent given to a proposition in which the Apprehension of the terms focuses more on them being mental concepts is referred to as Notional Assent. Real Assent will have a more specific relationship to the individual and particular beings of reality. On the other hand, Notional Assent relates more to the logical properties of the concepts existing in our minds. Newman explains: 'In its Notional Assents as well as in its inferences the mind contemplates its own creations instead of things; in Real, it is directed towards things, represented by the impressions which they have left on the imagination.'[10]

Notional Assent

Newman classifies Notional Assent into five different types. He bases his division on the nature of the Apprehension that is antecedent or concomitant with the Assent and refers to them as 'Profession, Credence, Opinion, Presumption, and Speculation'.[11]

Under the heading of 'Profession' come all Notional Assents that amount to rather superficial assertions, arising from the habit which the mind has of continually making spontaneous judgements with very little reflection. This kind of Assent is related to our familiarity with the fashions of the times, or from what is currently popular in the world at large. Usually they are little more than the echoes coming from the opinions of others. Sometimes they are Assents given to the conclusions of inferences whose premises we have accepted with very superficial Apprehension. It is 'professing to understand without understanding'.

'Credence' comprises those Notional Assents that are given on the grounds of general information with which we are in constant contact. They are also the consequence of the spontaneous character of the intellect which readily Assents to what seems reasonable. Credence is not accompanied with doubt, and such Notional Assents are the result of our general education and culture. They are usually derived from what we have learnt from others, rather than being the fruit of our own personal search for truth. They are 'the furniture of the mind'.

'Opinion' refers to the Notional Assent that is given to a proposition 'not as true, but as probably true, that is, to the probability of that which the proposition enunciates; and, as that probability may vary in strength without limit, so may the cogency and moment of the opinion'. While admitting that some might consider Credence and Opinion to be identical, he prefers to distinguish between them. He understands Opinion to imply a certain degree of intellectual reflection whereby our Assent is given to the probability of a particular proposition being true. On the other hand, Credence is Assent to a proposition where its truth is implicitly taken for granted. It is possible that, 'When we begin to reflect upon our credence, and to measure, estimate, and modify it, then we are forming an opinion.'[12] Opinion is always a Notional Assent since it implies that, included in 'the predicate of the proposition, on which it is exercised, is the abstract word "probable"'.

He defines 'Presumption' in the following terms: 'By presumption I mean an assent to first principles; and by first principles I mean the propositions with which we start in reasoning on any given subject matter.' These self-evident truths or first principles are the result of Notional Assents. However, it is vital to remember that 'Such notions indeed are an evidence of the reality of the special sentiments in particular instances, without which they would not have been formed; but in themselves they are abstractions from facts, not elementary truths prior to reasoning.'[13] Having already considered his view on

self-evident truths in an earlier chapter I will not dwell on them
any further. For his final category of Notional Assent he uses the word
'Speculation' 'to denote those notional assents which are the
most direct, explicit, and perfect of their kind, viz. those which
are the firm, conscious acceptance of propositions as true'.[14]
They are those which are only given after the most diligent
reflection and scientific investigation. It is worth bearing in
mind that he restricts this term Speculation to Notional Assents.

Real Assent

Real Assent is the act of Assent that is accompanied with Real
Apprehension: 'it is directed towards things, represented by the
impression which they have left on the imagination'. Real
Assent always implies a direct reference to some particular real
being or beings rather than just to concepts.

The *Grammar* describes various instances not only of the
different effects following on from these two kinds of Assent,
but also of the interplay between them. Those who began life
with a predominance of Notional Assents may, through personal
experience and natural talent, succeed in converting them into
Real Assents. He explains that 'These are the reformers, system-
atizers, inventors, in various departments of thought, speculative
and practical; in education, in administration, in social and political matters, in science.'[15]

He presents some examples showing how it is possible that,
'Great truths, practical or ethical, float on the surface of society,
admitted by all.' In such cases, however, it can happen that they
are only acknowledged in general with a kind of Notional
Assent. On the other hand, such a truth sometimes captures the
imagination of the majority due to 'changed circumstances,
accident, or the continual pressure of their advocates, force them
upon its attention'. Consequently, it may become generally
accepted with Real Assent. Such an appreciation of a truth with
Real Assent may lead to corporate action. He gives several
historical instances of such cases. Slavery, although generally

acknowledged as contrary to the dignity of man, needed a persistent and organized public campaign in order for this evil to be generally realized. And so slavery, as a consequence of this more general realization, was finally outlawed from European society. He also mentions the case of duelling, the evil of which had long been recognized as 'an abstract truth', as 'a notion without realizing the fact'. Nevertheless, it was not until the realization of this evil was brought home to the general public by 'the shock inflicted upon it by the tragical circumstances of a particular duel', that 'the duty of giving it practical expression' was finally undertaken.[16]

I have no doubt that if Newman was alive today he would have cited the tremendous impact of the mass media, especially in the form of visual images, in bringing home to large numbers of people a greater awareness, a Real Apprehension, of what is happening in other parts of the world. This realization is capable of changing public opinion into a general Real Assent that is capable of prompting action. For instance, the Real Assent to the suffering and plight of our fellow human beings on other parts of the globe can provoke a general response to provide practical help. What in the past was known only in a rather abstract way is now, as a result of the mass media, brought home to the general public in all its individual and particular reality. Such a conversion of Notional to Real Assents in the minds of many greatly facilitates real humanitarian assistance.

Our Real Assents can indirectly lead to subsequent human acts with respect to the situations around us. Since a Real Assent involves a deeper appreciation of reality it can provoke a definite response in one way or another. His distinction gives us a rather original way of explaining how certain realities have different effects on different people. Real Assent not only enriches the being of the knower but can also provide a constant source of inspiration for future action.

When our sense experience of reality enables us to make Real Assents it is usually accompanied with images produced in our imagination and memory. These in turn can exert a considerable influence on us, even when they have become disengaged from the original experience of reality that was their source. He cautions us against confusing such images produced by the imagination with reality itself: 'The fact of the distinctness of the images which are required for real assent, is no warrant for the existence of the objects which those images represent.'[17] We have already considered this danger of confusing the products of the imagination with those of the intellect. He also clarifies that, although the images from our memory or imagination may be involved in Real Assent, what is more likely to stimulate us to further action is 'hope and fear, likes and dislikes, appetite, passion, affection, the stirrings of selfishness and self-love'.[18]

He emphasizes the personal character of our Real Assents, 'each individual having his own, and being known by them'. With Notional Assent the situation is different: 'All of us have the power of abstraction, and can be taught either to make or to enter into the same abstractions; and thus to co-operate in the establishment of a common measure between mind and mind.'[19] It is easier for human beings to understand the propositions of Notional Assents and so they tend to form the basis of our communication.

On the other hand, since the propositions of Real Assent depend on personal experience of specific realities, they are prone to be more difficult to communicate to those who do not possess such experience. They are, however, essential in providing the foundations of our personal domain of knowledge. He explains:

> Till we have them, in spite of a full apprehension and assent in the field of notions, we have no intellectual moorings, and are at the mercy of impulses, fancies, and wandering lights, whether as regards personal conduct, social and political action, or religion.[20]

The ever-increasing number of Real Assents enriches the personality of the man or woman to whom they belong. At the same time, they provide a constant source of inspiration or incentive for future action. Newman concludes: 'They create, as the case may be, heroes and saints, great leaders, statesmen, preachers, and reformers, the pioneer of discovery in science, visionaries, fanatics, knight-errants, demagogues, and adventurers.' The more profound our knowledge of being, given through our Real Assents, the richer our own being becomes in knowledge. He goes on to say that when Real Assents are shared in common with others they can form the spirit of a nation, or the driving force of a movement.

In the section of the *Grammar* where he contrasts the nature of Real with that of Notional Assent he introduces the term 'Belief' as a synonym for Real Assent. Although, as he himself says, this term is valid for those propositions which we hold on the authority of another, it is rather confusing to use it to refer to all our Real Assents. It is possible that by using the word Belief in this context he wishes to stress the personal elements implied in giving a Real Assent. That is to say, he employs it according to popular usage. For instance in a proposition such as: I believe this statement, where this is equivalent to the Assent to the proposition: this statement is true. Such an Assent, as he explained earlier in his *Grammar*, will be a Real Assent since the predicate: is true, is apprehended with Real Apprehension.[21] Nevertheless, I feel that his use of the term Belief, as synonymous with Real Assent, without any further explanation can lead to misunderstanding.

He reaffirms that the difference between Notional and Real Assent does not lie in the act of Assent itself, which in either case is given unconditionally. The distinction is based on the antecedent and concomitant circumstances within which they come about. That is to say, Real Assent is derived from Real Apprehension whereas Notional Assent comes from Notional Apprehension. Also Real Assent, in contrast with Notional Assent, tends to be more conducive to a subsequent human response:

> Real Assent then, ... simply as Assent, does not lead to action; but the images in which it lives, representing as they do the concrete, have the power of the concrete upon the affections and passions, and by means of these indirectly become operative.[22]

Since the nature of the Assent to a proposition is dependant on that of its Apprehension thus a proposition may be affirmed by one person with Real Assent, while by another with Notional Assent. Furthermore, Notional Assents in the mind of an individual may become, as his experience of reality increases, Real Assents. He deals with this possible conversion of Notional Assent into Real Assent in his chapter entitled *Apprehension and Assent in the Matter of Religion*. I only consider one point that is of interest to his philosophy. He discusses the possible change of a Notional Assent to the existence of God as derived from rational arguments to, 'a real assent to the proposition that He exists'.[23] He explains that this can be achieved through an awareness of the reality of our conscience and its promptings. In turn this can lead us to have Real Apprehension of a personal living God, and so we may proceed to give a Real Assent to his existence. He clarifies that such a process may be quite independent from any knowledge of divine revelation, and so remains wholly within the domain of natural religion and reason. On the other hand, if divine revelation is accepted then this makes it possible to have Real Apprehension, and thus for the intellect to give a Real Assent to the existence of God.

His distinction between Notional and Real Assent shows his appreciation of the danger that our cognition could remain at the level of mental concepts. If this were to happen then our knowledge of reality would assume the form of a combination of concepts which only denoted the essences present in reality, but without necessarily knowing real, individual being, as such. Gilson warns us that in such a case there is a risk of our scientific and philosophical knowledge remaining in the realm of essential being, or just possible being.[24] Newman's distinction helps to avoid such a pitfall. Notional Assent affirms the reality of essences, allowing for their abstraction and separation from the individual or the various beings, to which they relate. However, as mentioned when discussing universals, reality is not just a complex pattern of essences. Our intellect is capable of knowing not just essences, but the individual beings which comprise reality, and to which these essences belong. The intellectual operation of Real Assent is our way of knowing individual reality. To know is to know the actual beings to which the essences belong. Referring to Real Assent in his *Grammar* he says that it:

> Has for its objects, not only directly what is true, but inclusively what is beautiful, useful, admirable, heroic; objects which kindle devotion, rouse the passions, and attach the affections; and thus it leads the way to actions of every kind, to the establishment of principles, and the formation of character, and is thus again intimately connected with what is individual and personal.[25]

I think that this distinction can have a practical value when it comes to philosophical discussion. It can be a safeguard against such a dialogue becoming totally abstract, resulting in arguments about possible being instead of dealing with reality.

I agree with Gilson when he stresses the importance of appreciating Newman's distinction between Real Assent and Notional Assent, since it is central to his approach to knowledge.[26] As with Apprehension, it is a distinction not of opposition but rather where the two forms of Assent are complementary. Gilson cautions that we must not think that 'notional assent is an imperfect form of real assent, or that, inversely, real assent is the completion or perfection of the notional assent'.[27]

Assent as Unconditional

Newman makes it abundantly clear that our acts of Assent are always given in an unconditional way. Apart from affirming it throughout the *Grammar* he also dedicates a separate chapter to this topic. In the opening paragraph he states his position: 'The circumstances of an act, however necessary to it, do not enter into the act; assent is in its nature absolute and unconditional, though it cannot be given except under certain conditions.'[28]

Care should be taken not to underestimate the importance that he attributes to this essential characteristic of Assent. Copleston appears to be a little dismissive when he refers to it in the following terms: 'In its most general form the statement that all assent is unconditional can hardly mean more than that assent is assent.'[29] The unconditional nature of Assent is an essential element of his theory of knowledge as opposed to Locke's view of there being 'degrees of assent'. Earlier in the *Grammar*, when discussing the effects of Apprehension on Assent, he already touched on this topic. He warned that due to the possible variation in the quality of our Apprehension we could be led into erroneously thinking that there was 'a scale of assents', ranging from vague opinion to absolute certainty.[30]

Both Sillem and Norris suggest that Newman's criticism of Locke is aimed at the general atmosphere of rationalism prevalent at the time, but singles him out in particular as typifying this tendency.[31] While quoting with respect from his famous work, *An Essay Concerning Human Understanding*, he exposes the inconsistencies he finds in his idea of Assent. For instance, he cites a passage where Locke is describing the qualities necessary in a person who is genuinely searching for truth:

I think, there is this one unerring mark of it, viz. *the not entertaining any proposition with greater assurance than the proofs it is built on will warrant.* Whoever goes beyond this measure of assent, it is plain, receives not truth in the love of it, loves not truth for truth-sake, but for some other by-end. For the evidence that any proposition is true (*except such as are self-evident*) lying only in the proofs a man has of it, whatsoever degrees of assent he affords it *beyond the degrees of that* evidence, it is plain *all that surplusage of assurance* is owing to some other affection, and not to the love of truth; it being as *impossible* that the love of truth should carry *my assent above the evidence* there is to me that it is true.[32]

At first sight this statement might lead us to think that Locke is simply cautioning us against making rash judgements, or asserting 'superstitious extravagances'. In other words, that the true scientist should have a healthy scepticism towards unproved hypotheses. This, of course, is good advice. However, a more careful consideration of this text shows that Locke is proposing that our assents exhibit a variation of degree in proportion to the evidence we possess for their justification. Newman considers such a view of Assent to be 'theoretical and unreal', a consequence of failing to distinguish between two distinct operations of the intellect, namely, Inference and Assent. Such confusion leads us into supposing that there exists a degree of Assent in proportion to the strength of the evidence for its justification. He explains that the logical consequence of Locke's theory, for those who 'love the truth', would be that they should only give their unconditional assent to the strictly self-evident truths, and to those conclusions derived from them through a strictly deductive demonstration. He concludes that such a theory would not only severely limit our sphere of knowledge, but also very easily lead to scepticism in some form or other.

He continues by showing that Locke is not consistent with his own theory, he cannot ignore the 'logic of facts', and again quotes an example taken from his *Essay*:

> Most of the propositions we think, reason, discourse, nay, act upon, are such as we cannot have undoubted knowledge of their truth; yet some of them *border so near* upon certainty, that we *make* no doubt at all about them, but *assent* as resolutely, *as if they were infallibly demonstrated*, and that our knowledge of them was perfect and certain.[33]

He explains how, in this example as with respect to others, Locke is effectively stating that we do, in practice, Assent to propositions whose evidences only amount to probabilities. Thus he contradicts his own 'arbitrary theory': 'He consults his own ideal of how the mind ought to act, instead of interrogating human nature as an existing thing, as it is found in the world.'[34]

His criticism of Locke and those of the same school gives us, as Fey also observes, one more insight into his realism.[35] The Assent of the intellect is 'absolute and unconditional' because it is an affirmation of the truth of the relationship between the content of the mental assertion and reality, or to that aspect of it, to which it refers. Newman affirms: 'We might as well talk of degrees of truth as of degrees of assent.' The mind either gives its Assent to a proposition as true, or suspends its judgement due to insufficient evidence: 'There is no medium between assenting and not assenting.'[36]

The unconditional nature of Assent does not mean therefore that all our Assents are certitudes. As we have seen he divides Notional Assent into five possible categories, ranging from what he calls 'Profession' to 'Speculation'. In each case Assent is given unconditionally. However, the different kinds of Notional Assent arise from the concomitant or antecedent conditions under which they are given. Thus, with respect to 'Opinion', the proposition of such an Assent implies that, in the final analysis, its predicate can be reduced to: 'is probable'.[37] It is this probability factor that determines that such an Assent is not held as a certitude. However, the Assent itself remains absolute and unconditional as an act of the intellect.

There is some evidence showing a development in his thought regarding the unconditional nature of Assent. In some notes written in May 1853 on the certainty of faith, he divides Assent into 'absolute' and 'conditional'.[38] Nevertheless, by the end of that same year in additional notes on the same subject he clearly states: 'An assent does not admit of degrees.'[39]

Following his refutation of Locke's theory on degrees of Assent he presents his own reasons for concluding that this act of the intellect is always unconditional. He argues that, as witnessed by the psychological facts, Inference and Assent as 'operations of the intellect' are 'intrinsically distinct', and 'they are not always found together'. We are able to distinguish clearly between the conclusion of an Inference and the proposition of an Assent. This is shown by the fact that Assents persist even after the Inferences, or evidence on which they were given, have been forgotten. On the other hand, we may find that we are now not able to give our Assent to a proposition that, some time previously, we were able to do so even though the evidence on which it was grounded is still valid. This suggests that certain moral factors have a bearing on Assent. There is also the case where the reasons, provided by convincing Inferences, may increase and become ever more conclusive. Nevertheless, 'the assent either exists or does not exist'. On occasions Inferences may accumulate, pointing more and more clearly to the veracity of a particular conclusion. However, an individual may freely refuse to give his Assent to it 'according to the couplet', which Newman quotes: 'A man convinced against his will, Is of the same opinion still.'[40]

He says that 'strange as it may seem, this contrast between inference and assent is exemplified even in the province of mathematics'. Sometimes it can be difficult, especially when there are many steps in a logically correct demonstration, to actually give our Assent to the conclusion without a great mental effort. He wishes to stress that Inferences indicate conclusions which are conditional, at least they depend on the truth of their premises. On the other hand, Assent is always given, or denied, in an unconditional way. Assent is the intellectual operation through which we know:

> If assent is the acceptance of truth, and truth is the proper object of the intellect, and no one can hold conditionally what by the same act he holds to be true, here too is a reason for saying that assent is an adhesion without reserve or doubt to the proposition to which it is given.[41]

He describes some of the many daily instances when, on being presented with information of a most varied nature and from diverse sources, we simply suspend our judgement and do not give our Assent. At the same time, we do not talk of giving a degree of Assent. He mentions how, when we talk of Opinion, we do not refer to 'variations of assent to an inference, but assents to a variation in inferences'. Assent to a proposition, which we judge only to have a probability of being true, still remains unconditional. This is because our Assent is given to the complete proposition which includes the reference to probability in its predicate.

He discusses the many cases where we give Assent, even though it is only based on 'probable reasoning'. We are given another glimpse of his realist approach when he states that he is not considering the topic 'according to *à priori* fitness, but according to the facts of human nature, as they are found in the concrete action of life'.[42] After affirming once again that 'there is no medium between assent and no assent', he presents a series of examples of propositions to which we usually give an unconditional Assent. These propositions are in themselves neither self-evident, nor the result of deductive Inferences, nor indeed borne out by direct sense experience. Amongst such Assents he mentions the following: the Assent to the planet earth being a 'globe'; 'that there are vast tracts on it of land and water'; that we had parents; that we shall die; that the world has had a history; and so on. He says that, in giving our Assent to such propositions, we do not 'think ourselves guilty of not loving truth for truth's sake, because we cannot reach them through a series of intuitive propositions'. He then concludes:

> Assent on reasonings not demonstrative is too widely recognized an act to be irrational, unless man's nature is irrational, too familiar to the prudent and clear-minded to be an infirmity or an extravagance. None of us can think or act without the acceptance of truth, not intuitive, not demonstrated, yet sovereign.[43]

He reiterates that any possible confusion lies in mistaking the inferential arguments, which may exhibit a certain probability, with the actual mental act of Assent: 'It is the mind that reasons and assents.' Certain everyday expressions used in connection with Assent may contribute to the misunderstanding of its unconditional nature. However, when they are given a little thought it is seen clearly that they refer to the circumstances under which the Assent was made, and not to there being any degree in Assent. This is the case with expressions like, 'deliberate assent', 'rational assent', 'sudden', 'impulsive', or 'hesitating' Assent. In a similar way it may seem that Assents, given to propositions grounded on historical evidence or made on the authority of another, exhibit a certain degree of strength or weakness, which may even vary over time. He answers that:

> When we carefully consider the matter, it will be found that this increase or decrease of strength does not lie in the assent

itself, but in its circumstances and concomitants; for instance, in the emotions, in the ratiocinative faculty, or in the imagination.[44]

The unconditional nature of Assent is an essential property of this intellectual operation and central to Newman's approach to knowledge. Furthermore, it is important in showing that our Assent is a personal affirmation of a proposition as true. It is a free and responsible act on the part of the person who Assents. Ward, referring to this topic, concludes that: 'This is perhaps the newest and subtlest contribution to the problem.'[45]

Complex Assent

Newman also introduces another distinction regarding Assent. This time it is based on whether our Assent is made after a conscious intellectual reflection of the proposition under consideration, or not. He says that many of our Assents are given 'unconsciously', in a spontaneous way without us being aware of any intellectual reflection. They are the consequence of our already acquired mental habits. He designates these as 'simple' Assents. Conversely, those 'made consciously and deliberately' he refers to as 'complex or reflex assents'.[46]

A simple Assent can become a complex Assent after being subjected to an 'investigation' of the grounds on which it is held. In the case of success the simple Assent is reiterated as a complex Assent. Such an investigation does not involve the rejection of our initial Assent; it is 'not *ipso facto* to doubt its truth'. Once again we see his aversion to the so-called methodical doubt. Complex Assent implies investigation and intellectual reflection regarding the evidence supporting the original Assent. He distinguishes between this 'investigation' and 'inquiry'. The latter refers specifically to those operations of the intellect involved in proceeding from a lack of knowledge to knowing, but where no Assent has been given so far. The investigation of a simple Assent does not always result in its re-affirmation as a complex Assent. If it reveals error then Assent will be denied.

Such an occurrence should not lead us to doubt all our simple Assents until they can be investigated and reiterated as complex Assents. The fact that many of our simple Assents do, in the course of time, become complex Assents is due to our ongoing education and intellectual development throughout life.

This distinction between simple and complex Assent also seems to reflect the thought of Aquinas. Simple Assent is that given to a proposition without any conscious intellectual reflection, the result of our already existing knowledge and acquired habits of intellect. Conversely, complex Assent is the consequence of a deliberate investigation by the intellect. In the case of Real Assent the conversion from simple to complex Assent entails a return (*reditio*), to investigate the sense experience or reality from which it was derived, with the possibility of an increase in our knowledge.[47]

Certitude

In his *Apologia* Newman affirms: 'To be certain is to know that one knows.'[48] The question of certitude is an essential element with regard to the theological purpose of his *Grammar*. He wishes to show that it is not irrational to Assent with certitude to the truths proposed by divine revelation. In philosophical terms, however, the problem is how to explain the possibility of certitude with respect to propositions that cannot be adequately demonstrated by strictly logical Inference. In notes of 1853 he had already outlined his view on this topic mainly in the context of religious faith.[49] After his discussion on simple and complex Assent in the *Grammar* he introduces the concept of certitude:

> I have one step farther to make – let the proposition to which the assent is given be as absolutely true as the reflex act pronounces it to be, that is, objectively true as well as subjectively: then the assent may be called a *perception*, the conviction a certitude, the proposition or truth a certainty, or thing known or a matter of *knowledge*, and to assent to it is to *know*.[50]

In a later chapter dealing with his concept of the 'Illative Sense' he gives a concise summary of his view on certitude:

> Certitude is a mental state: certainty is a quality of propositions. Those propositions I call certain, which are such that I am certain of them. Certitude is not a passive impression made upon the mind from without, by argumentative compulsion, but in all concrete questions (nay, even in abstract, for though the reasoning is abstract, the mind which judges of it is concrete) it is an active recognition of propositions as true, such as it is the duty of each individual himself to exercise at the bidding of reason, and, when reason forbids, to withhold. ... Every one who reasons, is his own centre.[51]

Certitude is 'an active recognition' of the intellect as opposed to it being imposed by external arguments. It is a state of mind as a consequence of a free and deliberate act of complex Assent for which the individual is entirely responsible. He describes two conditions of the mind for certitude. In the first place, that 'no one can be called certain of a proposition, whose mind does not spontaneously and promptly reject, on their first suggestion, as idle, as impertinent, as sophistical any objections which are directed against its truth'.[52] On the other hand, that:

> It is accompanied, as a state of mind, by a specific feeling, proper to it, and discriminating it from other states, intellectual and moral, I do not say, as its practical test or as its *differentia*, but as its token, and in a certain sense its form.[53]

This 'token' implies 'a sentiment *sui generis* in which it lives and is manifest', an 'intellectual security', 'special relaxation and repose of mind'. He does not consider this 'specific feeling' that accompanies certitude to be a guarantee as to its truth. It does not represent a criterion for truth in any Cartesian sense. It is a 'token', a sign that the conditions for certitude appear to be fulfilled.

He provides various examples regarding these two conditions, comparing and contrasting them with other possible states of mind, and showing their uniqueness in the case of certitude. He concludes his phenomenological description saying, 'That Certitude is a natural and normal state of mind', just as there are other characteristic sentiments corresponding to other states of mind.[54]

Apart from these introductory remarks there is a separate chapter in the *Grammar* where certitude is dealt with in more depth. He considers the phenomenon whereby 'simple assent' can be considered as 'virtual, material or interpretive certitude' in the sense that, if it were to be investigated it would become the complex Assent of certitude. However, only in the event that this does happen can the original simple Assent then be designated as a 'virtual certitude'.[55] Our certitude with respect to a proposition is a complex Assent that has some 'confirmatory' phrase as a predicate added to the proposition of the simple Assent, such as, 'is beyond all doubt'. In some draft notes for the *Grammar* he explains that certitude:

> As being the assertion of a correspondence between what is without and what is within me, it involves a recognition of myself. Thus it differs from knowledge, which is the simple contemplation of truth as objective. Hence we speak of having knowledge and feeling certain.[56]

Certitude implies a proposition where the predicate includes a 'confirmatory' phrase. According to its nature such a phrase is only capable of Notional Apprehension. Therefore, certitude is always a Notional Assent. By way of example he proposes the proposition: 'That "the cholera is in the midst of us" is beyond all doubt.' As a Notional Assent it lacks that 'bearing upon action' and the 'freshness and vigour' characteristic of Real Assent. This of course also applies if the original simple Assent was a Notional Assent. Nonetheless, certitude will always have that 'repose of mind' and the 'depth and exactness' of the 'reflex confirmation'. At the same time, since the simple Assent still remains in the mind after its conversion into a complex Assent its possible influence towards future action will still be present if it was a Real Assent. This is the case with the example he gave earlier where the simple Real Assent is, 'the cholera is in the midst of us'. Thus the resulting combination of Real Assent and certitude can exhibit both a 'keenness' together 'with repose and persistence'.[57]

Another characteristic of certitude is 'indefectibility'. Since the object of certitude is truth as known with a complex Assent and 'Truth cannot change; what is once truth is always truth; ... therefore once certitude, always certitude. ... it carries with it an inward assurance, strong though implicit, that it shall never fail. Indefectibility almost enters into its very idea.' If certitude did not possess this essential property then our ability to know the truth would be in jeopardy. Thus he affirms:

> It is of great importance then to show, that, as a general rule, certitude does not fail; that failures of what was taken for certitude are the exception; that the intellect, which is made for truth, can attain truth, and, having attained it, can keep it, can recognize it, and preserve the recognition.[58]

At the same time, he openly admits that there seems to be so much evidence against this 'indefectibility' that perhaps we should 'be content with probability, as the true guide of life, renouncing ambitious thoughts' of certitude. He explains the distinction between 'indefectibility' and 'infallibility'. The intellectual operation of Assent is not infallible, it can err. Certitude is 'a disposition of mind relatively to a definite' complex Assent. It is 'a deliberate assent given expressly after reasoning'. If in the future it is found to be false then, 'It is the reasoning that is in fault, not my assent to it. It is the law of my mind to seal up the conclusions to which ratiocination has brought me, by that formal assent which I have called a certitude.' Subsequent failure of our certitudes should not deter us from formulating new ones:

> Errors in reasoning are lessons and warnings, not to give up reasoning, but to reason with greater caution. It is absurd to break up the whole structure of our knowledge, which is the glory of the human intellect, because the intellect is not infallible in its conclusions.[59]

The history of science provides ample evidence for this conclusion. What was thought to have been certain yesterday is today shown not to be entirely correct. This may occur as a consequence of new evidence coming to light confirming an alternative theory. For instance, in the scientific debate about the origin of the universe we have seen how the 'big bang theory' has supplanted that of the 'constant state theory' on account of later astronomical observations. Alternatively, a hitherto unknown error may be discovered in the reasoning process that invalidates the original conclusion. In such cases it is usually clear that it was not a failure of certitude as such. What becomes apparent is that the original conclusion should not have been held with certitude in the first place, since a deepening in our knowledge of reality now reveals that it was only probable. As Ker points out, we must not exaggerate the value that Newman gives to his concept of the 'indefectibility' of certitude; he is only claiming it as a general rule.[60]

It is our rational nature itself that provides the warrant for our certitudes. He says that mistaken certitudes are not 'sufficient to constitute a proof, that certitude itself is a perversion or extravagance'.[61] He suggests that in many cases error is the consequence of not recognizing the difference between 'the probable, the possible, and the certain'.[62] What was affirmed with certitude in the first place had, in fact, no right to such a claim. The domain of our certitudes is small in comparison with what we should more correctly designate as Opinions. He remarks that, since on many occasions we are obliged by circumstances to act on our Opinions, 'Hence it is that – the province of certitude being so contracted, and that of opinion so large – it is common to call probability the guide of life.'[63] Nevertheless, as he explains, this maxim does not apply in all cases since we do experience certitude with some of our complex Assents. The most obvious certitudes are, for example, those with respect to self-evident truths and first principles.

The remainder of his chapter on certitude is devoted to the application of his conclusions in the field of religious truth. Since this does not concern us I limit myself to some remarks regarding his philosophical argument. He clarifies that in the case of religion we are dealing, not with 'a proposition, but a system' of propositions. As such it will be made up of a collection of 'various kinds of assents', and not all of them will be held as certitudes. The important question is to explain how it is that on occasions some certitudes fail, they cease to be, or are replaced by others. Cases exist, as a consequence of the addition of new certitudes, where there can even be a change of religion. The original ones 'remain unimpaired, or rather confirmed' by such a transition. Alternatively, the failure of some certitudes may also result in the affirmation of a different religion. He suggests that in such cases the likelihood is that some of the original beliefs were not in fact held as certitudes, and thus were always susceptible to change. They may only have been 'prejudices, ... which will not bear careful examination'.[64] Therefore, a change under such circumstances is not due to a failure in certitudes.

In the closing paragraphs of his chapter on certitude he reiterates some of his conclusions. For instance, that certitude does not have 'an interior, immediate test, sufficient to discriminate it from false certitude'. Also, that the 'indefectibility' of certitude 'may at least serve as a negative test of certitude, or *sine qua non* condition, so that whoever loses his conviction on a given point is thereby proved not to have been certain of it'. And finally he summarizes his three basic conditions for certitude: 'That it follows on investigation and proof, that it is accompanied by a specific sense of intellectual satisfaction and repose, and that it is irreversible.'[65]

Newman's uncompromising stance on the unconditional nature of the act of Assent begs the following question. How can we explain that, in certain cases, an unconditional complex Assent is given to a proposition where the rational evidence for its justification, at best, only indicates the probability of it being true? He is well aware, as he himself tells us, that a solution is needed for 'the apparent inconsistency which is involved in holding that an unconditional acceptance of a proposition can be the result of its conditional verification'.[66] Although he presents us with examples to illustrate that the evidence of everyday life shows that there is no contradiction in fact, it is only later in his *Grammar* that he answers this question.

Notes

1. *GA*, p. 12 (7).
2. *GA*, p. 10 (5).
3. *TP* I, p. 64.
4. Aquinas, *Summa Theologiae* I, q. 16, a. 1.
5. *GA*, p. 169 (259); cf. *Phil N* II, pp. 71–3; *TP* I, p. 11.
6. *GA*, p. 128 (195–6); cf. *TP* I, p. 127.
7. Cf. *TP* I, p. 11.
8. *GA*, p. 16 (13).
9 Cf. *GA*, pp. 31–2 (36–8).
10. *GA*, p. 55 (77).
11. *GA*, p. 35 (43).
12. *GA*, p. 45 (59).
13. *GA*, p. 49 (65).
14. *GA*, p. 54 (73).
15. *GA*, p. 55 (76).
16. *GA*, p. 56 (77–8).
17. *GA*, p. 58 (80).
18. *GA*, p. 59 (82).
19. *GA*, p. 60 (83).
20. *GA*, p. 63 (88).
21. Cf. *GA*, pp. 16–19 (13–18).
22. *GA*, p. 63 (89).
23. *GA*, p. 73 (105).
24. Cf. Gilson, *Elements of Christian Philosophy*, p. 253; ibid., *Unity of Philosophical Experience*, p. 68.
25. *GA*, p. 64 (90–1).
26. Cf. Gilson, 'Introduction', in *GA* (1955), p. 15.
27. Gilson, 'Introduction', in *GA* (1955), p. 14.
28. *GA*, p. 105 (157).
29. Copleston, vol. VIII, p. 523.
30. *GA*, p. 30 (35).
31. Cf. Sillem, p. 25; Norris, pp. 4–5.
32. *GA*, p. 108 (162–3). Newman quotes from the 18th edn, p. 382.
33. *GA*, pp. 106–7 (161).

34. *GA*, p. 109 (164).
35. Cf. Fey, p. 10.
36. *GA*, p. 116 (176).
37. Cf. *GA*, p. 45 (60).
38. *TP* I, p. 11.
39. *TP* I, p. 32.
40. *GA*, p. 112 (169).
41. *GA*, p. 114 (172).
42. *GA*, p. 116 (176).
43. *GA*, p. 118 (179).
44. *GA*, p. 122 (185).
45. Ward, vol. II, p. 246.
46. *GA*, p. 124 (189).
47. Cf. Aquinas, *Summa Theologiae* I, q. 84, a. 7; ibid., *De Veritate*, q. 2, a. 6 ad 3.
48. *Apo*, p. 228.
49. Cf. *TP* I, pp. 31–6.
50. *GA*, p. 128 (195–6); cf. *TP* I, pp. 31–2.
51. *GA*, p. 223 (344–5); cf. *TP* I, pp. 122, 126.
52. *GA*, p. 129 (197).
53. *GA*, p. 134 (204); cf. *TP* I, p. 126; *Diffs* I, p. 79.
54. *GA*, p. 137 (209).
55. *GA*, p. 139 (212–13).
56. *TP* I, p. 127.
57. *GA*, p. 142 (216).
58. *GA*, p. 145 (221–2).
59. *GA*, p. 150 (230).
60. Cf. Ker, 'Introduction', in *GA* (1985), pp. lxix–lxx.
61. *GA*, p. 152 (233).
62. *GA*, p. 153 (234).
63. *GA*, p. 155 (237).
64. *GA*, p. 166 (254).
65. *GA*, p. 168 (258).
66. *GA*, p. 105 (157).

CHAPTER 5

INFERENCE

Newman's view on the difference between the intellectual operations of Inference and Assent is one of the cornerstones of his *Grammar*. Scholars such as Ward, W. De Smet, Norris and Ker agree that it is a crucial distinction on which hinges his approach to knowledge.[1] The idea came to him like an Archimedean eureka. It happened in August 1866 while in Switzerland. He was there to rest on medical advice. He described the event in the following way: 'At last, when I was up at Glion over the lake of Geneva, it struck me "You are wrong in beginning with certitude – certitude is only a kind of assent – you should begin with contrasting assent and inference".'[2] This came as a real breakthrough after searching for many years for such an insight with respect to his work on religious faith and reason.[3] He says that it gave him 'the point from which to begin';[4] 'the clue, the "Open Sesame", of the whole subject'[5] that four years later saw the light as his *Grammar*.

He begins his chapter on Inference by affirming the difference between the intellectual operations of reasoning and Assent: 'Inference is the conditional acceptance of a proposition, Assent is the unconditional; the object of Assent is a truth, the object of Inference is the truth-like or a verisimilitude.' He then states the aim of this chapter:

The problem which I have undertaken is that of ascertaining how it comes to pass that a conditional act leads to an unconditional; and, having now shown that assent really is unconditional, I proceed to show how inferential exercises, as such, always must be conditional.[6]

That is to say, the value of our Inferences, of whatever kind, as instruments in our quest for knowledge depends on various conditioning factors. At the same time, it is only the act of Assent that affirms as true, or denies as false, their conclusions in an unconditional way.

He then explains the mind's ability to reason: 'By means of sense we gain knowledge directly; by means of reasoning we gain it indirectly, that is by virtue of previous knowledge.'[7] In the preface to the third edition of his *University Sermons*, published in 1872, he provides a complementary definition: 'By Reason is properly understood any process or act of the mind, by which, from knowing one thing, it advances on to know another.'[8]

Formal Inference

In our quest for a universal and thoroughly reliable 'instrument of reasoning (that is, of gaining new truths by means of old)' different kinds of reasoning have developed that can be expressed in terms of words or symbols. He designates these kinds of reasoning as 'Formal Inference'. As examples of such Inference he cites those found in geometry, algebra and logic, and concludes: 'Ratiocination, thus restricted and put into grooves is what I have called Inference, and the science, which is its regulating principle, is Logic.'[9] In his lecture notes on logic, that have already been referred to on several occasions, he clarifies:

> The Science of Proof or Inference ... an instrument which we use whether we are discussing questions of history, of politics, of commerce, of mathematics, or of mechanics. It follows from this that it is not concerned with the truth or falsehood of the subject matter, but is hypothetical. The only truth it is concerned with is that of the act of inference. And

its object is truth of inference, and its occupation is the determination of the laws of true or correct inference.

By 'inference' is meant the process of the mind to what is unknown from, besides, and because of what is known. A is true, therefore B is true. If A is true, B is true, or vice versa, B is true, because A is true, B is true supposing A is true which is called 'proof'.[10]

Newman affirms that, in the final analysis, a Formal Inference can be converted into the 'Aristotelic syllogism'. In fact all 'verbal reasoning, of whatever kind, as opposed to mental, is what I mean by inference, which differs from logic only inasmuch as logic is its scientific form'. He says that:

> Logical inference ... proposes to provide both a test and a common measure of reasoning; and I think it will be found partly to succeed and partly to fail; succeeding so far as words can in fact be found for representing the countless varieties and subtleties of human thought, failing on account of the fallacy of the original assumption, that whatever can be thought can be adequately expressed in words.[11]

Formal Inference is instrumental in helping us to reach new truths and to communicate them to others, provided we can find the appropriate words or symbols to express our concepts. This condition represents a clear disadvantage when we wish to reach truth with respect to concrete reality through Formal Inference. Those concepts that are the product of Notional Apprehension, that are more abstract, can be represented more accurately in appropriate words for Formal Inference. Conversely, those resulting from Real Apprehension are more difficult to put into words, while at the same time preserving their ontological richness. Thus, in the process of the different steps in the Formal Inference the terms representing individual realities, contained in the various propositions, may lose something of their ontological precision. He explains:

> The nearer the propositions concerned in the inference

approach to being mental abstractions, and the less they have to do with the concrete reality, and the more closely they are made to express exact, intelligible, comprehensible, communicable notions, and the less they stand for objective things, that is, the more they are the subjects, not of real, but of notional apprehension, – so much the more suitable do they become for the purposes of Inference.[12]

In other words, the symbolic representation of our concepts can fall short in conveying, with an ontological completeness, the reality contained in the concept present in our mind. To appreciate his argument it is vital to notice that he is focusing his attention in particular on Inference, not so much in enabling us to know essences, but to increase our knowledge about individual realities:

> Abstract can only conduct to abstract; but we have need to attain by our reasonings to what is concrete; and the margin between the abstract conclusions of the science, and the concrete facts which we wish to ascertain, will be found to reduce the force of the inferential method from demonstration to the mere determination of the probable.[13]

He then considers the fact that the validity of all Inferences depend on the truth of their first premises. A Formal Inference may be very complicated, consist of many steps and be dependent on other preliminary Formal Inferences. In every case, however, they can all be traced back to a set of first premises from which the entire syllogistic process began. The validity of the whole system of Formal Inferences will stand or fall on the truth of these premises. As we have already seen, these premises are our self-evident truths and first principles: 'propositions with which we start in reasoning on any given subject matter'.[14]

Given that the premises are true, and that the logical development of the Formal Inference is correct, then its conclusion will be true. In other words, the truth of a conclusion to a Formal Inference is conditional on that of its premise. These premises, however, may be 'accepted by some, rejected by others'.

Furthermore, when the Formal Inference is very elaborate with many supplementary independent arguments, then the situation is aggravated by the presence of many more premises. This increases the risk that some of them may not be considered as true by everybody. Consequently, regardless of the faultless logic of the argument, Assent to the conclusion will not be given by all or, at best, it will only be an Assent to its probable truth.

Newman concludes that, when Formal Inference is used to establish truth regarding individual reality:

> Logic then does not really prove; it enables us to join issue with others; it suggests ideas; it opens views; it maps out for us the lines of thought; it verifies negatively; it determines when differences of opinion are hopeless; and when and how far conclusions are probable; but for genuine proof in concrete matter we require an *organon* more delicate, versatile, and elastic than verbal argumentation.[15]

At this point in his *Grammar* he does not say explicitly what this other '*organon*' is, but proceeds to illustrate his explanation with an example. He considers the value of Formal Inference in the domain of literature when used to prove the authenticity of a text supposedly written by William Shakespeare. That is to say, to establish a truth regarding a concrete reality. He maintains that, however thorough and exact the arguments may be in arriving at a conclusion, it will not necessarily be agreed upon by all. This will be due to the multiplicity of premises and presumptions that are involved in such a verbal demonstration. The resulting conclusion would only be acceptable by those who also held as true all the premises on which the overall argument is based.

He then proceeds to show that, independent of the premises, the conclusion of Formal Inference in conditional. This is due to the intellectual abstraction involved in the formulation of the propositions that constitute the Formal Inference. And, as we have just seen: 'Abstract can only conduct to abstract; but we have need to attain by our reasonings to what is concrete.' He illustrates this with an example taken from the field of 'mathematical physics'. Referring to the discovery of the planet

Neptune in 1846 he remarks that: 'It was deservedly considered a triumph of science, that abstract reasonings had done so much towards determining the planet and its orbit.' This was because, one year previously, the existence of such a planet had been predicted by means of mathematical calculations. He then comments: 'There would have been no triumph in success, had there been no hazard of failure.' If the conclusions of the Formal Inferences, on which these predictions were based, had been considered as certain then there should have been no surprise when they were verified by observation. He also adds that our trust in engineers and navigators is not just because of their ability to apply their science, but because of their experience in practice: 'That reasoning by rule should be completed by the living mind.' Newman concludes: 'Science, working by itself, reaches truth in the abstract, and probability in the concrete; but what we aim at is truth in the concrete.'[16]

Leaving the world of mathematical physics he goes on to consider Formal Inferences in general. He suggests that many 'come to no definite conclusions about matters of fact, except as they are made effectual for their purpose by the living intelligence which uses them'. He explains how, since their propositions involve abstractions from specific aspects of reality, thus their conclusions, applied to a particular case in reality, may not in fact be true. Their conclusions are probable rather than necessary. Using examples of premises such as 'all men are rational', he says that the Formal Inference based on such a premise may fail with respect to a particular man, 'for he may be an idiot'. He then clarifies: 'Since, as a rule, men are rational, progressive, and social, there is a high probability of this rule being true in the case of a particular person; but we must know him to be sure of it.'[17]

In the final analysis Newman is affirming that Formal Inference is limited when it tries to reach truth with respect to individual reality. In such cases their conclusions are conditional, and they can only determine a certain probability. In this assertion it is important to remember that he is referring strictly to the conclusions of Formal Inference as such. At this stage he is not contemplating the fact that it is the human mind that actually does the reasoning and, as a consequence of all the available evidence, gives or refuses its Assent to any conclusion being true with respect to a particular case in reality.[18]

Given the spirit of rationalism current at the time, it is not surprising that his insistence on Formal Inference only being able to reach probable conclusions with respect to concrete reality provoked criticism. In 1885 Andrew Martin Fairbairn (1838–1912) accused him publicly of scepticism in an article published in the *Contemporary Review*.[19] The crux of his argument rested on the meaning that Newman had given to the term 'Reason'. He answered Fairbairn in the next issue of the same journal stating that he had used it in the popular sense.[20] That is to say, as that which differentiates humans from animals, rather than its more philosophical sense which limits its meaning to strictly deductive reasoning. In a subsequent fuller reply he gives a definition of scepticism: 'The system which holds that no certainty is attainable, as not in other things so not in questions of religious truth and error.'[21] It is sufficient to remember his understanding of 'certitude', as portrayed in the *Grammar*, to appreciate that scepticism has no place in his philosophy.

Even today some authors, like Philip Flanagan, have criticized Newman for what they consider to be his demeaning attitude towards Formal Inferences when it comes to determining truth regarding individual reality.[22] However, as Artz rightly points out, this is not the case.[23] On the contrary, Newman extols 'the uses of this logical inference':

It is the great principle of order in thinking; it reduces a chaos into harmony; it catalogues the accumulations of knowledge; it maps out for us the relations of its separate departments; it puts us in the way to correct its own mistakes. ... Nor is it a slight benefit to know what is probable, and what is not so, what is needed for the proof of a point, what is wanting in a theory, how a theory hangs together, and what will follow, if it be admitted. Though it does not itself discover the unknown, it is one principal way by which discoveries are made.[24]

Later in his *Grammar* he elaborates more on the value of Formal Inference:

> Great as are the services of language in enabling us to extend the compass of our inferences, to test their validity, and to communicate them to others, still the mind itself is more versatile and vigorous than any of its works, of which language is one, and it is only under its penetrating and subtle action that the margin disappears, which I have described as intervening between verbal argumentation and conclusions in the concrete.[25]

He also comments on the fact that naturally and spontaneously, 'We think in logic, as we talk in prose, without aiming to do so.' This enables us to express ourselves in a more objective way and to justify our conclusions to others: 'Thus inference becomes a sort of symbol of assent, and even bears upon action.'[26] Nevertheless, it is only instrumental in enabling us to Assent to its conclusions. It is through our unconditional Assent that we advance in knowledge.

Newman's understanding of Formal Inference, when dealing specifically with concrete reality, as only resulting in conclusions that in themselves are conditional or probable, in contrast with the act of Assent being unconditional, concurs with the philosophical tradition following Aquinas. For instance, Gilson expresses it in the following terms:

> Logic in itself is the science and the art which concerns the formal conditions of judgments in general. As such, it is directly concerned with the formal validity of judgments, not with their actual truth. Unless a judgment be correct, it cannot be true, but it can be correct without being true. If a judgment aims to be true, it aims, beyond formal and purely logical correction, to achieve an adequate expression of actually existing reality.[27]

In his discussion on Formal Inference Newman tends to use examples within the realm of deductive reasoning. Consequently there is a certain risk of the casual reader thinking that by 'Formal' he excludes all arguments that are not strictly deductive. On the contrary, it is important to notice that by Formal Inference he includes 'all inferential processes whatever, as expressed in language'. Therefore, together with deductive demonstrations, he includes reasoning based on 'Induction and Analogy'.[28] Judging by his use of the term induction, both in the *Grammar* and in the rest of his writings, it is clear that he gives it the same meaning as was then current in the world of science, namely, as referring to scientific demonstration.[29] Thus he includes induction within the domain of Formal Inference and formal logic.[30] In an earlier chapter we saw that in the *Grammar* he distinguishes clearly between 'induction' and 'intuition'. The latter being the ability of the intellect to apprehend self-evident truths and first principles.

His writings do not contain any detailed explanation about his understanding of scientific or empirical induction. Nevertheless, there are some general references. In some notes of 1853, dealing with certainty in religious faith, he compares deductive reasoning with that of induction 'under the head of truths ... which are in *contingent* matter, ... are gained ... by *induction*, those which are reached, ... by a complex argument consisting of accumulating and converging probabilities'. With respect to 'whether they can make up a proof' which is sufficient, he affirms, 'I have no doubt' that they can. He also clarifies that he does not 'hold the analysis of the process of induction ... as it is described by Whewell or by Mill, viz I do not think that induction is a necessary proof or demonstration'.[31] We will see later how some of the terminology and concepts used here become part of his view on Informal Inference. In these same notes he also distinguishes between 'intuition' and 'induction'. By way of example of the latter he refers to the scientific explanation of Newton's laws of motion given by James Wood in his book, *The Principles of Mechanics*.[32] He gives this same example in the *Grammar* as an illustration of Informal Inference.

From what can be gathered from his writings there does not seem to be anything in Newman's view on induction, as a scientific demonstration, contrary to that found in the tradition of

Aquinas. Empirical or scientific induction, based on the principle of causality as its premise, as a consequence of experimental investigation and empirical experience of certain effects concludes that they are the result of a certain cause or causes. That is to say, the existence of a physical law is demonstrated through its known effects; a scientific explanation in terms of causes is found for these effects. By introducing a proposition based on the principle of causality it is always possible to express such a demonstration in a syllogistic form. For instance, a syllogism can be constructed where the major premise enunciates that certain effects imply a particular cause or causes. In this way a categorical syllogism can be expressed, for example: someone with these symptoms has malaria; John has these symptoms; therefore, John has malaria. An all-important factor to be taken into account is that physical causes do not produce their effects necessarily. That is to say, such effects follow under certain conditions.

These characteristics are also found in Newman's notion of scientific induction. He considers it to fall within the context of Formal Inference on the basis that, in the final analysis, all demonstrations can be expressed in syllogistic form.[33] We have seen in a previous chapter that, when referring to causality with respect to physical causes, he prefers to talk of the 'order in Nature ... the fact that things happen uniformly according to fixed circumstances, and not without them or at random: that is, that they happen in an order'. In some of his notes he mentions explicitly that this is one of 'the first principles involved in induction'.[34] At the same time he stresses that 'The order of nature is not necessary, but general in its manifestations.' The so-called laws of nature do not exclude the possibility of exceptions, they 'are not inviolable truths; much less are they necessary causes'. In a comment he makes on Mill's *System of Logic*, referring to the uniformity of the laws of nature, he stresses the '*ordinary* uniformity' as opposed to Mill who appears to attribute an absolute necessity to this uniformity.[35]

He ends the section on Formal Inference in the *Grammar* by repeating the idea that he has being trying to stress throughout. When conclusions of Formal Inference refer directly to individual reality then, as such, they fall short of affirming certainty and always imply a degree of probability: 'I have assumed ... that all verbal argumentation is ultimately syllogistic; and in consequence that it ever requires universal propositions and comes short of concrete fact.'[36]

Informal Inference

The term Informal obviously does not suggest any lack of due rigour in this kind of inference. Newman uses it to indicate the contrast with Formal Inference. Formal implies that the Inference is expressed in words or in some other symbolic form. On the other hand, Informal Inference refers directly to all inferential processes as occurring in the mind, and not necessarily as being enunciated. This includes both those that may incidentally be expressed as Formal Inferences and those that seem to defy being adequately expressed in some form or other. Later in his *Grammar* he refers to Formal Inference simply as, 'the logic of language', and to Informal Inference as, 'the logic of thought'.[37]

He commences his explanation of Informal Inference by boldly announcing that it is:

> The method by which we are enabled to become certain of what is concrete; ... It is the cumulation of probabilities, independent of each other, arising out of the nature and circumstances of the particular case which is under review; probabilities too fine to avail separately, too subtle and circuitous to be convertible into syllogisms, too numerous and various for such conversion, even were they convertible.[38]

In order to avoid misunderstanding it is worth dwelling on what he means in this context by 'probabilities'. He is referring to the probable nature of the individual items of rational evidence, understood in the widest possible sense, that are presented to our intellect as a warrant for our Assent. Each piece of independent evidence points towards a particular conclusion. They all indicate in a probable way the possible veracity of this conclusion, and therefore individually are referred to as probabilities. That is to say, such evidences, taken separately, are only probable indicators with respect to the truth of a conclusion. Such probabilities may be derived from self-evident truths, first principles, empirical evidence, or the conclusions of all forms of inference and scientific demonstrations. They may also include evidences accepted on the authority of others. However, if Assent is finally given to a conclusion on the strength of all these probabilities then, as with all our Assents, it is made unconditionally. In other words, Assent is given to the conclusion indicated by the various pieces of evidence which, if taken separately on their own, would only point to the likelihood of the conclusion being true. In a letter he comments: 'My main proposition, in my Essay is, that by the nature of the human mind we assent absolutely on reasons which taken separately are but probabilities.'[39]

It is clear that Newman is not using probability in the sense that was used by Butler in his aphorism, 'Probability is the guide of life.' Referring to this expression in his *Apologia* he writes: 'The danger of this doctrine, in the case of many minds, is, its tendency to destroy in them absolute certainty.'[40] Likewise, the term probable with regard to Informal Inference is not to be confused with its meaning in mathematics. It is not a measure of quantity nor does it imply proportion. It should be understood in the sense of implying that such a conclusion is feasible or conditional, in some way, rather than considered as being necessary.

From very early in his career at Oxford Newman gave importance to this kind of reasoning. For example, various aspects of it are already present in his *University Sermons*. At this time he frequently referred to it using the expression 'antecedent probabilities'. He described it in terms of the 'grounds which do not reach so far as to touch precisely the desired conclusion, though they tend towards it, and may come very near it'.[41] He even mentions that this idea was one of the most original concepts found in his *Sermons*.[42] There is some evidence to show that on this topic he was influenced by Whately who, in one of his books, spoke of probabilities which '*gradually approach* indefinitely near to the case supposed'.[43] In Newman's *Development of Christian Doctrine* 'antecedent probabilities' become the very 'method of proof'.[44]

In his *Grammar* he proposes Informal Inference as the form of reasoning that enables us to attain truth with respect to reality in its individuality: 'This I conceive to be the real reasoning in concrete matters.'[45] He also considered it to be one of the more important elements of his science of knowledge portrayed in the *Grammar*.[46]

Informal Inference has three characteristics: 'First, it does not supersede the logical form of inference, but is one and the same with it; only it is no longer an abstraction, but carried out into the realities of life.' The second is, 'that such a process of reasoning is more or less implicit, and without the direct and full advertence of the mind exercising it'. He suggests an analogical comparison with our sense experience. Our senses detect similarities or differences in our observations of reality without the necessity of any explicit act of reflective analysis being apparent to us. Its third characteristic is, as with Formal Inference, that its conclusions are conditional, being 'dependent on premisses'. There are also other factors that make the situation more complex. He explains:

A cumulation of probabilities, over and above their implicit character, will vary both in their number and their separate estimated value, according to the particular intellect which is employed upon it. It follows that what to one intellect is a proof is not so to another, and that the certainty of a proposition, does properly consist in the certitude of the mind which contemplates it.[47]

He proceeds to discuss three rather mundane examples of propositions that are accepted by most people as certitudes, and yet seem to defy being demonstrated by Formal Inference. On the other hand, when considered as conclusions derived from Informal Inference, the majority of us find it relatively easy to give to them an Assent of certitude. These propositions deal with contingent reality and refer respectively 'to the present, the past, and the future'.

The first is one that appears quite frequently in his writings, namely, the proposition: 'Great Britain is an island.'[48] He says that our reasons for assenting to this proposition as a certitude are usually based on testimony derived from very many sources and that, 'There is a manifest *reductio ad absurdum* attached to the notion that we can be deceived on such a point as this.' We judge the evidence available to us as quite sufficient to be able to give our Assent to this conclusion with certitude.

His second illustration is taken from the field of historical investigation regarding literary sources. He considers the hypothesis that certain classical works, attributed to authors such as Virgil, Horace, Livy, Tacitus and Terence, are the invention of medieval forgers. The grounds for such an hypothesis are that we do not possess their original manuscripts, but only copies dating from the medieval period. He suggests that the argument depends on whether or not the medieval intellect had the ability to create such forgeries. However, having taken into account all the available evidence, he then concludes that: 'We feel sure that at least it could not write the classics. An instinctive sense of this, and a faith in testimony, are the sufficient, but the undeveloped argument of which to ground our certitude.'[49]

He expresses his final example in the form of a question, 'what are my grounds for thinking that I, in my own particular case, shall die?' He explains that in terms of Formal Inference we can only arrive at a probable conclusion for such a future event. And in any particular case there is no absolute necessity that it will occur: 'The strongest proof I have for my inevitable mortality is the *reductio ad absurdum*.' He concludes that:

> But what logic cannot do, my own living personal reasoning, my good sense, which is the healthy condition of such personal reasoning, but which cannot adequately, express itself in words, does for me, and I am possessed with the most precise, absolute, masterful certitude of my dying some day or other.[50]

He ends his discussion of these three examples by saying that: 'Many of our most obstinate and most reasonable certitudes depend on proofs which are informal and personal, ... and cannot be brought under logical rule.' As we have just seen, both in the first and last of these examples he refers to the '*reductio ad absurdum*' argument. Later in the *Grammar* he returns to consider this principle as being an essential aspect of Informal Inference. In particular he mentions how the 'law-books tell us that the principle of circumstantial evidence is the *reductio ad absurdum*'.[51] With respect to Informal Inference this principle represents the situation where, to deny the conclusion towards which all the rational evidence is pointing, would imply certain contradictions within my existing circle of knowledge.

After considering the general nature of Informal Inference he explains its specific mode of operation. He compares it to the way our senses, in the first instance, tend to perceive reality in terms of whole entities before observing and differentiating the details:

> Such too is the intellectual view we take of the *momenta* of proof for a concrete truth; we grasp the full tale of premises and the conclusion, *per modum unius*, – by a sort of instinctive perception of the legitimate conclusion in and through the premises, not by a formal juxta-position of propositions; though of course such a juxta-position is useful and natural, both to direct and to verify.[52]

He sees Informal Inference not so much as a discursive, linear form of reasoning as in the case of Formal Inference, but rather as implying a kind of multi-linear approach. Each independent line of argument points to the same probable conclusion. The mind has the ability of maintaining a unified view, '*per modum unius*', of the whole process. It is able to consider in a unified way all these different lines of rational evidence as they focus on a possible conclusion. The intellect can dwell on an hypothetical conclusion within the context of all the evidences and inferences which could possibly have some bearing on it. Thus a moment may come when it is able to judge that the accumulation of all this rational evidence in favour of a particular conclusion is sufficient as a proof for its veracity. And, as a consequence, the intellect is able to give its unconditional Assent to this conclusion.

Since Informal Inference takes place wholly in the mind it can easily be appreciated that its operation is affected by certain subjective factors, such as, the ability of the person to judge correctly and his or her intellectual integrity. Referring to these aspects he says: 'our criterion of truth is not so much the manipulation of propositions, as the intellectual and moral character of the person maintaining them, and the ultimate silent effect of his arguments or conclusions upon our minds.'[53]

He presents seven different illustrations of how such personal factors can influence our Informal Inferences. His first is with respect to a discussion on how best to understand a political statement such as: '"We shall have a European war, *for* Greece is audaciously defying Turkey".' His last example is of a philosophical argument to show that God possesses the attribute of knowledge. After discussing these examples he concludes:

> Here then again, as in the other instances, it seems clear, that methodical processes of inference, useful as they are, as far as they go, are only instruments of the mind, and need, in order to their due exercise, that real ratiocination and present imagination which gives them a sense beyond their letter, and which, while acting through them, reaches to conclusions beyond and above them. Such a living *organon* is a personal gift, and not a mere method or calculus.[54]

This time it is quite clear that with the term '*organon*' he is referring to Informal Inference. It seems to me that he uses this word quite deliberately in order to put us in mind of Aristotle's understanding of logic. Later in his *Grammar*, when he comes to describe 'Natural Inference', he openly criticizes Aristotle for what he considers to be his rather narrow view on reasoning. It appears that Newman thought that it only comprised what he designates as Formal Inference: 'In spite of Aristotle, I will not allow that genuine reasoning is an instrumental art.'[55]

He continues his explanation of Informal Inference by arguing that, in practice, it is universally accepted. Even earlier in the *Grammar* he had alluded to this fact:

> Assent on reasonings not demonstrative is too widely recognized an act to be irrational, unless man's nature is irrational, too familiar to the prudent and clear-minded to be an infirmity or an extravagance. If our nature has any constitution, any laws, one of them is this absolute reception of propositions as true, which lie outside the narrow range of conclusions to which logic, formal or virtual, is tethered.[56]

He also calls upon Locke, who admitted the existence of such a mental process for some of our truths, as a witness to the validity of Informal Inference. Newman takes a much broader view and affirms that:

> They are to be found throughout the range of concrete matter, and that supra-logical judgment, which is the warrant for our certitude about them, is not mere common-sense, but the true healthy action of our ratiocinative powers, an act more subtle and more comprehensive than the mere appreciation of a syllogistic argument. It is often called the 'judicium prudentis viri', a standard of certitude which holds good in all concrete matter, ... in questions of truth and falsehood generally, or in what are called 'speculative' questions, and that, not indeed to the exclusion, but as the supplement of logic. Thus a proof, except in abstract demonstration, has always in it, more or less, an element of the personal, because 'prudence' is not a constituent part of our nature, but a personal endowment.[57]

Our language reveals the general acceptance in practice of Informal Inference:

> We are considered to feel, rather than to see, its cogency; and we decide, not that the conclusion must be, but that it cannot be otherwise. We say that we do not see our way to doubt it,

that it is impossible to doubt, that we are bound to believe it, that we should be idiots, if we did not believe.[58]

The use of such expressions as these shows that:

We have arrived at these conclusions not *ex opere operato*, by a scientific necessity independent of ourselves, – but by the action of our own minds, by our own individual perception of the truth in question, under a sense of duty to those conclusions and with an intellectual conscientiousness.[59]

He gives two further instances of Informal Inference. In the first, taken from the field of astronomy, he says that Samuel Vince employs just such an argument to demonstrate the rotation of the earth.[60] In the second he suggests that Butler, in his *Analogy*, also uses this form of reasoning to show the existence of divine revelation.[61] On comparing these two examples he concludes:

Here, as in Astronomy, is the same absence of demonstration of the thesis, the same cumulating and converging indications of it, the same indirectness in the proof as being *per impossibile*, the same recognition nevertheless that the conclusion is not only probable, but true.[62]

He then poses the hypothetical question as to whether 'any account can be given of the ratiocinative method in such proofs, over and above that analysis into syllogism which is possible in each of its steps in detail'. After answering in the affirmative he introduces quite a different and ingenuous kind of illustration to show how he thinks Informal Inference operates. It is clearly one of the fruits of his interest and love for mathematics. He proposes the basic concept of Newton's differential calculus as a model of how Informal Inference works in practice:

I consider, then, that the principle of concrete reasoning is parallel to the method of proof which is the foundation of modern mathematical science, as contained in the celebrated lemma with which Newton opens his 'Principia'. We know that a regular polygon, inscribed in a circle, its sides being continually diminished, tends to become that circle, as its limit; but it vanishes before it has coincided with the circle, so that its tendency to be the circle, though ever nearer fulfillment, never in fact gets beyond a tendency. In like manner, the conclusion in a real or concrete question is foreseen and predicted rather than actually attained; foreseen in the number and direction of accumulated premises, which all converge to it, and as the result of their combination, approach it more nearly than any assignable difference, yet do not touch it logically, (though only not touching it,) on account of the nature of its subject-matter, and the delicate and implicit character of at least part of the reasonings on which it depends.[63]

That is to say, just as this mathematical method consists in the gradual convergence towards a particular result indicated when certain values are taken to a limit, so the verification of the conclusion of an Informal Inference is given as being the limit of converging probabilities: 'A proof is the limit of converging probabilities.' As in the case of Formal Inference, this conclusion remains only as probable until the intellect actually gives its Assent to it as true.

To avoid misunderstanding it is worth giving careful consideration to Newman's use of this mathematical model taken from Newton's *Principia mathematica*. He is not claiming that the operation of Informal Inference is identical to this mathematical method, but rather, that it is similar in an analogical way. He says that it 'is parallel to the method of proof which is the foundation of modern mathematical science'. It is certainly a very useful analogy in helping us to understand the basic principle of Informal Inference. Not only is it easy to visualize, but also this mathematical principle provides us with an appropriate way of understanding how Informal Inference functions.

We are presented with the geometrical diagram of an equal-sided polygon inscribed within a circle whose angular points touch the circumference. We are then asked to consider that the sides of this regular polygon are multiplied by making the length of the sides progressively shorter while its angular points still touch the circumference. As this process continues the outer contour of the polygon approaches closer and closer to the circumference of the circle, such that it 'tends to become that circle, as its limit'.

It seems clear to me that Newman, as a mathematician, is not just offering us a visual aid, but is asking us to consider the importance of the mathematical principle itself. It is at the beginning of his *Principia* that Newton lays the foundations for the theory of differential and integral calculus. This new branch of mathematics became an important element of 'modern mathematical science'. It revolutionized many aspects of applied mathematics, the theoretical sciences and even economic theory.

He proceeds with his explanation of Informal Inference adding that: 'The logical form of this argument, is, as I have already observed, indirect, viz. that "the conclusion cannot be otherwise".' In other words, the logical basis of Informal Inference is the principle of *reductio ad absurdum*. Again he turns to the mathematical analogy in support of his explanation:

> So Newton too is forced to the same mode of proof for the establishment of his lemma, about prime and ultimate ratios. 'If you deny that they become ultimately equal,' he says, 'let them be ultimately unequal;' and the consequence follows, 'which is against the supposition'.[64]

Three examples are provided to illustrate the intellectual operation of Informal Inference. In the first he refers to the scientific explanation of Newton's 'laws of motion' given by Wood in his book, *The Principles of Mechanics*.[65] He comments:

> The reasoning of this passage (in which the uniformity of the laws of nature is assumed) seems to me a good illustration of what must be considered the principle or form of an induction. The conclusion, which is its scope, is, by its own confession, not proved; but it ought to be proved, or is as good as proved, and a man would be irrational who did not take it to be virtually proved.[66]

It is only 'as good as proved' as a consequence of the imperfections inherent in the experiments available to demonstrate these laws. However, when these experiments are refined the results show an even closer approximation to Newton's Laws. Furthermore, 'When the conclusion is assumed as an hypothesis, it throws light upon a multitude of collateral facts, accounting for them, and uniting them together in one whole.' This consistency, although it 'is not always the guarantee of truth', reinforces the claim of veracity for the conclusion.

His second illustration of Informal Inference in action is the gradual accumulation of circumstantial evidence in a court of law. Each piece of evidence, taken independently, is not sufficient to prove the case. However, when all this evidence is viewed together as a whole it can be seen as focusing on one conclusion. It can provide sufficient grounds, beyond reasonable doubt, for assenting to this conclusion as true.

The final instance is taken once more from the field of literary investigation. He considers how the scholar, from the internal evidence provided by the writings of an anonymous author, may be able to establish the identity of the writer on the basis of converging probabilities. At the same time, the expert would confess 'that a logical argument could not well be made out for it'.[67] In such a case it is clear that the scholar is able to assent to the conclusion due in part to the expertise that he has attained in his particular area of research.

It seems to me that neither Aristotle nor Aquinas would find anything serious to disagree with regarding Newman's account of Informal Inference. He is not proposing some new operation of the intellect, but rather trying to emphasize the supremely personal nature of all reasoning. Nobody can reason for us, even though 'paper logic' can serve us well in making explicit our 'logic of thought', and in enabling us to communicate our arguments to others. In his *Apologia* he says: 'I had a great dislike of paper logic ... It is the concrete being that reasons.'[68] As we have seen, Informal Inference makes use of all the operations of the intellect with the advantage that, taking place in the mind, the intellect can be continually monitoring and reflecting on the whole process, '*per modum unius*', while gathering all the relevant rational evidence. This takes on a specific importance when a conclusion is sought with respect to concrete reality.

As already mentioned, there will be no advance in knowledge unless there is a personal Assent to either the conclusions of Formal Inference, or to those of Informal Inference. It is the individual person who must freely decide whether or not there are, for him, sufficient grounds for making an Assent to any particular conclusion as true. All acts of Assent are unconditional. When such conclusions refer to individual reality then, inherent in both forms of Inference, there is always a certain element of probability. As we have seen, our Assent is still unconditional even if it is to a proposition which includes in its predicate some phrase indicating probability. Informal Inference comes into its own when we are trying to determine truth with respect to concrete individual reality.

In a private letter Newman suggests a useful metaphor to distinguish between Formal and Informal Inference. Referring to Informal Inference he says that: 'The best illustration ... is that of a *cable* which is made up of a number of separate threads, each feeble, yet together is sufficient as an iron rod.' He then adds that the latter 'represents mathematical or strict demonstration' as in Formal Inference.[69]

Artz affirms that several aspects of this distinction have 'produced an essentially new contribution to epistemology'.[70] In particular he says it shows that: 'Arguing and reasoning are not identical.' Informal Inference takes place entirely in the mind and is characterized precisely by the fact that it cannot be adequately expressed in terms of 'paper logic'. In other words, reasoning belongs to the person as such, whereas 'arguing' represents an attempt at a reflective justification of our reasoning in terms of Formal Inference.

Natural Inference

In the *Grammar* Newman distinguishes a third form of Inference that he designates as 'Natural Inference'. He calls it Natural simply because it is 'an existing phenomenon of the mind':

Reasoning ordinarily shows as a simple act, not as a process, as if there were no medium interposed between antecedent and consequent, and the transition from one to the other were of the nature of an instinct, – that is, the process is altogether unconscious and implicit. ... our most natural mode of reasoning is, not from propositions to propositions, but from things to things, from concrete to concrete, from wholes to wholes.[71]

The intellect learns to function by habit, without any necessary consciousness of the operation by which it arrives at a conclusion. This natural process takes place in the mind both of the genius and in those who lack any formal education. Its ability to actually arrive at truth appears in some cases to be a natural gift, and in others it has been acquired by long experience and practice. Due to its nature a person may not be able to give an adequate scientific account of the reasons that led him to a particular conclusion. Newman describes Natural Inference in the following terms:

It is a power of looking at things in some particular aspect, and of determining their internal and external relations thereby. And according to the subtlety and versatility of their gift, are men able to read what comes before them justly, variously, and fruitfully. ... We determine correctly or otherwise, as it may be; but in either case it is by a sense proper to ourselves, for another may see the objects which we are thus using, and give them quite a different interpretation, inasmuch as he abstracts another set of general notions from those same phenomena which present themselves to us also.[72]

Since it is the consequence of a habit of the mind it usually shows itself as more successful in one 'definite subject-matter, according to the individual'. Appealing to the universal experience of mankind Newman suggests that genius with respect to reasoning tends to be confined to specific fields of knowledge. By way of example he says:

> No one would for a moment expect that because Newton and Napoleon both had a genius for ratiocination, that, in consequence, Napoleon could have generalized the principle of gravitation, or Newton have seen how to concentrate a hundred thousand men at Austerlitz. The ratiocinative faculty, then, as found in individuals, is not a general instrument of knowledge, but has its province, or is what may be called departmental.[73]

He compares the effectiveness of Natural Inference with that of memory. The memories of different people vary, not just with respect to the content of their experience, but also as to their ability to recall that experience in some spheres of knowledge with more precision than in others. Similarly, the ability of any individual, to attain knowledge through Natural Inference, will differ according to his experience and antecedent knowledge in specific fields of learning. To illustrate this point he quotes from Aristotle's *Nicomachean Ethics*:

> We are bound to give heed to the undemonstrated sayings and opinions of the experienced and aged, not less than to demonstrations; because, from their having the eye of experience, they behold the principles of things.[74]

He concludes that to 'gain that mental insight into truth' which our 'masters' possessed we must 'follow their history, and learn as they have learned' from a profound and long experience of that aspect of reality which was the object of their study.

Ker notices that one of Newman's *University Sermons* already includes elements of his concept of Natural Inference.[75] In it he speaks of 'Implicit Reason' and says that the mind is able to affirm a conclusion as true without necessarily being able to produce a cogent logical argument as its warrant:

> In other words, all men have a reason, but not all men can give a reason. We may denote, then, these two exercises of mind as reasoning and arguing, or as conscious and unconscious reasoning, or as Implicit Reason and Explicit Reason.

And to the latter belong the words, science, method, development, analysis, criticism, proof, system, principles, rules, laws, and others of a like nature. ... The process of reasoning is complete in itself, and independent. The analysis is but an account of it; it does not make the conclusion correct; it does not make the inference rational.[76]

Thus, in the *Grammar*, Newman divides Inference into three kinds, Formal, Informal and Natural. In simple terms this division is based on whether the Inference can be expressed in terms of 'the logic of language', or that it cannot be exhaustively expressed, and remains as 'the logic of thought'. The former being designated as Formal Inference while the latter includes both Informal and Natural Inference. These last two are differentiated on the grounds that Natural Inference takes place in the mind in an entirely spontaneous, unreflective way, derived from the habit that the intellect acquires from experience and possible training. He fully recognizes the value of Formal Inference in its ability to express with precision the logical justification for the more abstract, notional and speculative truths. However, it is essential to Newman's theory of knowledge to remember that, with respect to any of these forms of Inference, it is only the mind itself that is able to relate, through a Real Assent, any of their conclusions to individual beings in reality; that can know concrete reality: 'It is the mind that reasons, and that controls its own reasonings, not any technical apparatus of words and propositions.'[77]

Towards the end of his section on Natural Inference he refers to this form of reasoning as 'this illative faculty'.[78] And then, after discussing the importance of personal experience and training in knowing concrete reality, in the very last paragraph of this chapter he concludes: 'Judgment then in all concrete matter is the architectonic faculty; and what may be called the Illative Sense, or right judgment in ratiocination, is one branch of it.'[79] In this way he introduces the all important element of his theory of knowledge that will be the subject of his next chapter.

Notes

1. Cf. Ward, vol. II, pp. 245–6; De Smet, p. 31; Norris, pp. 29–30; Ker, *John Henry Newman. A Biography*, p. 647.
2. *AW*, p. 270.
3. Cf. Ward, vol. II, pp. 245–6, 270, 278; De Smet, p. 31; Ker, 'Introduction', in *GA* (1985), pp. xxxiii–xxxiv; Ker, *John Henry Newman. A Biography*, pp. 618–23.
4. *LD* XXV, p. 35.
5. *LD* XXV, p. 199.
6. *GA*, p. 169 (259); cf. *TP* I, p. 135.
7. *GA*, pp. 169–70 (260); cf. *US*, p. 256.
8. *US*, p. xi; cf. ibid., p. 223.
9. *GA*, p. 171 (263).
10. *TP* I, p. 53; cf. ibid., p. 55.
11. *GA*, p. 172 (264).
12. *GA*, p. 172 (265).
13. *GA*, p. 175 (268); cf. ibid., pp. 66–7 (94).
14. *GA*, p. 45 (60).
15. *GA*, p. 176 (271).
16. *GA*, p. 181 (279); cf. *Idea*, pp. 46–7.
17. *GA*, p. 182 (280).
18. Cf. *GA*, pp. 185 (284–5), 196 (302), 204–5 (315–16), 227–8 (353).
19. Cf. Fairbairn, 'Catholicism and Modern Thought', *The Contemporary Review*, 47 (1885), pp. 652–74.
20. Cf. Newman, 'The Development of Religious Error', *The Contemporary Review*, 48 (1885), pp. 457–69. It is included in *TP* I, pp. 140–9; cf. ibid., pp. 47, 149–57; *US*, pp. xi, 198–9, 216.
21. *TP* I, p. 150; cf. ibid., pp. 8–10.
22. Cf. Flanagan, pp. 97–8.
23. Cf. Artz, 'Newman as Philosopher', pp. 274–5.
24. *GA*, p. 186 (286).
25. *GA*, p. 232 (360); cf. ibid., p. 233 (363).
26. *GA*, p. 186 (287).
27. Gilson, *Being and Some Philosophers*, p. 200.
28. *GA*, p. 184 (283).
29. Cf. *GA*, pp. 184–5 (283–4), 209 (323); *Idea*, pp. 49, 223, 224, 441; *TP* I, pp. 19, 41, 44–5, 65, 93–4.
30. Cf. *TP* I, p. 53.
31. *TP* I, p. 19; cf. ibid., pp. 18–19, 65.
32. Wood, p. 31.

Inference 119

33. Cf. *GA*, pp. 184 (283), 187 (287) footnote 1.
34. *TP* I, p. 93.
35. *TP* I, p. 45.
36. *GA*, p. 187 (288) footnote 1; cf. ibid., p. 189 (291).
37. *GA*, p. 231 (359).
38. *GA*, p. 187 (288).
39. *LD* XV, p. 456.
40. *Apo*, pp. 30–1; cf. ibid., p. 19.
41. *US*, p. 224; cf. ibid., pp. xii, 187–9, 203, 204, 213, 223, 232, 252–3, 264, 273, 297; *Mir* I, pp. 67, 73, 177.
42. Cf. *LD* XI, p. 293.
43. Whately, *Elements of Rhetoric*, p. 56.
44. Cf. *Dev*, chapter 3 (section 1), pp. 100–1, 106, 110, 112, 123, 142, 327.
45. *GA*, p. 189 (292).
46. Cf. *LD* XIV, p. 348; *LD* XXV, p. 266.
47. *GA*, p. 190 (293).
48. *GA*, p. 191 (294); cf. ibid., pp. 119 (181), 124 (189), 128 (195); *PS* I, p. 195; *TP* I, pp. 20, 87–9, 129; *LD* XII, p. 440; *LD* XVIII, pp. 334; 471; *LD* XXIV, p. 315.
49. *GA*, p. 193 (297).
50. *GA*, p. 195 (300–1); cf. *TP* I, p 20.
51. *GA*, p. 208 (322).
52. *GA*, p. 196 (301).
53. *GA*, p. 196 (302).
54. *GA*, p. 205 (316).
55. *GA*, p. 219 (338).
56. *GA*, p. 118 (179).
57. *GA*, p. 205 (317); cf. ibid., p. 247 (383); cf. *TP* I, pp. 24–6, 30, 36–8, 90.
58. *GA*, p. 206 (317).
59. *GA*, p. 206 (317).
60. Vince, pp. 84, 85.
61. Butler, pp. 329, 330.
62. *GA*, p. 207 (319–20).
63. *GA*, pp. 207–8 (320–1); cf. Newton, *Philosophiae naturalis principia matematica*, book 1, lemma I: 'Quantities, and the ratios of quantities, which in any finite time converge continually to equality, and before the end of that time approach nearer to each other than by any given difference, become ultimately equal.' Quotation is taken from *Sir Isaac Newton's Mathematical Prin-*

ciples of Natural Philosophy and his System of the World, p. 29.
64. *GA*, p. 208 (322).
65. Wood, p. 31.
66. *GA*, p. 209 (323); cf. *Dev*, p. 123; *TP* I, pp. 19, 44–5.
67. *GA*, p. 212 (328).
68. *Apo*, p. 155.
69. *LD* XXI, p. 146.
70. Artz, 'Newman as Philosopher', pp. 274–5.
71. *GA*, pp. 213–14 (330).
72. *GA*, p. 218 (337–8).
73. *GA*, p. 219 (339).
74. *GA*, pp. 220–1 (341–2); Aristotle, *Nicomachean Ethics*, book VI, xi, 6.
75. Cf. Ker, 'Introduction', in *GA* (1985), p. xxxi.
76. *US*, p. 259; cf. *TP* I, p. 43; *Phil N* II, pp. 29, 35, 73, 75, 130.
77. *GA*, p. 227 (353); cf. ibid., pp. 196 (302–3), 205 (316).
78. *GA*, p. 215 (333).
79. *GA*, p. 221 (342).

CHAPTER 6

THE ILLATIVE SENSE

I think most Newman scholars would still agree with Ward who, writing in 1912, said that: 'The doctrine of the "illative sense" has become by general consent the most characteristic lesson taught by the "Essay".'[1] In 1947 Charles Harrold echoed the same sentiments when he said, referring to the Illative Sense in his introduction to an edition of the *Grammar*, that it was 'by general consent the most striking lesson taught by the *Grammar*'.[2] In a private letter Newman comments that it is simply 'a grand word for a common thing'.[3]

Without doubt the Illative Sense is one of the major concepts in his approach to knowledge. In a nutshell it is that aspect of the intellect that comes into play when a particular conclusion, whether it be the result of Formal, Informal or Natural Inference, comes before the intellect for possible Assent. It is our Illative Sense that enables us to give or deny Assent to that conclusion. It certifies, as it were, that the conclusion is worthy of Assent; that it is indeed reasonable to give Assent to this proposition.

The chapter that discusses this key concept of his science of knowledge begins by reiterating his conclusions with regard to certitude. 'The common voice of mankind' is a sufficient warrant for our being able to attain certainty in knowledge. That is to say, 'Our possession of certitude is a proof that it is not a weakness or an absurdity to be certain.' He repeats that he is primarily concerned with our certitude of the 'truth of things', of determining truth regarding concrete reality rather than with respect to universals. 'Certitude is a mental state' in which there is 'an active recognition of propositions as true'. It is only the individual intellect that can Assent with certitude on the grounds of all the available rational evidence: 'Every one who reasons, is his own centre.' He introduces that aspect of the intellect which fulfils this role with the following words: 'The sole and final judgment on the validity of an inference in concrete matter is committed to the personal action of the ratiocinative faculty, the perfection or virtue of which I have called the Illative Sense.'[4]

In the *Grammar*, instead of the term Illative Sense, he sometimes uses expressions like, 'right judgment in ratiocination',[5] the 'power of judging and concluding, when in its perfection',[6] he even refers to it simply as, 'the reasoning faculty'.[7] He explains that with respect to Illative Sense he uses 'the word "sense" parallel to our use of it in "good sense", "common sense", a "sense of beauty", etc.' Walgrave suggests that Newman possibly had in mind the meaning given to this term by Thomas Reid.[8] As Ker points out, it is clear that by employing the word 'sense' he intends his term Illative Sense to imply an active rather than a passive role with respect to Assent.[9]

The fundamental role of the Illative Sense is to enable us to reach truth regarding concrete individual reality. Consequently, it is feasible that he also uses the term 'sense' in an analogical way to the operation of the external senses in perceiving individual reality. At the same time it is a word that seems to highlight the personal element involved in the act of Assent.

Existence and Nature

After giving a rough sketch of his notion of the Illative Sense he proceeds to present a rational justification for its existence. He bases his argument on the teleological nature of the universe. The contemplation of reality reveals the existence of a certain order which tends to be self-perpetuating, and where different beings have real relationships of dependence one with the other. This kind of functionality, purpose or finality, is more clearly observed within the world of living beings. They possess within themselves all that is necessary for their own development according to their nature, while at the same time serving the good and well-being of other living beings, and the physical world as a whole. Furthermore, even inanimate beings seem to cooperate in producing the necessary conditions for the development of life and in maintaining an overall stability.

Within this context Newman explains that rational beings also form part of this teleological pattern and follow their own nature which is to 'our interest as well as our necessity'. However, 'in contrast with the inferior animals', the human person 'is a being of progress with relation to his perfection and characteristic good'. He continues:

> Man begins with nothing realized (to use the word), and he has to make capital for himself by the exercise of those faculties which are his natural inheritance. Thus he gradually advances to the fullness of his original destiny. Nor is this progress mechanical, nor is it of necessity; it is committed to the personal efforts of each individual of the species; each of us has the prerogative of completing his inchoate and rudimental nature, and of developing his own perfection out of the living elements with which his mind began to be.[10]

The next step in his argument is to point out that this 'progress is carried out by means of the acquisition of knowledge, of which inference and assent are the immediate instruments'. And, if we consider our nature as we actually find it functioning in practice, then we must conclude that:

> There is no ultimate test of truth besides the testimony borne to truth by the mind itself, and that this phenomenon, perplexing as we may find it, is a normal and inevitable characteristic of the mental constitution of a being like man on a stage such as the world. His progress is a living growth, not a mechanism; and its instruments are mental acts, not the formulas and contrivances of language.[11]

He also appeals to the providence of God as a warrant that he would not permit us to be deceived when we experience the characteristic feeling of certitude.

Before going on to examine the nature of the Illative Sense he gives another brief description of it: 'It is the mind that reasons, and that controls its own reasonings, not any technical apparatus of words and propositions. This power of judging and concluding, when in its perfection, I call the Illative Sense.'[12]

He compares this specific role of the intellect with what he refers to as 'parallel faculties, which we commonly recognize without difficulty'. The first comparison is with our ability to judge with respect to everything that in some way is relevant to the achievement of our own personal good. He refers to the *Nicomachean Ethics* of Aristotle who designates the term 'φρόνησις' to refer to this capability of the intellect to make correct moral judgements.[13] '*Phronesis*' has the nature of an acquired virtue that enables an individual to pursue his personal wellbeing. He says that 'an ethical system may supply laws, general rules, guiding principles, a number of examples', but it is our *phronesis* that enables us to make a here and now decision. Furthermore, it is that 'from which the science of morals forms its rules and receives its complement'.

Newman is not claiming that the Illative Sense is the same as *phronesis*: 'In this respect of course the law of truth differs from the law of duty, that duties change, but truths never.' He is only comparing their respective roles analogically. The Illative Sense operates in an analogous way to *phronesis*, not regarding our personal good, but with respect to truth. In a footnote he clarifies that Aristotle did not consider *phronesis* 'in its general relation to truth and the affirmation of truth'.[14] The Illative Sense is that function of the intellect that enables us to integrate and evaluate all the evidence, together with the conclusions of our inferences, with respect to the likelihood of a particular conclusion being true. At the same time, it gives the sanction for affirming or refusing Assent to this conclusion. When such a conclusion refers to individual reality the operation of the Illative Sense can be seen in a more evident way. It determines the conclusion given in 'the limit of the converging probabilities and the reasons sufficient for a proof'.[15] Newman, in a letter of 1879 intended for his friend

Froude, gives a brief description of the Illative Sense in which he refers to it as the 'inductive sense'. He continues by saying that it is similar to Aristotle's *phronesis*, 'its province being, not virtue, but the "inquisitio veri", which decides for us, beyond any technical rules, when, how, etc. to pass from inference to assent, and when and under what circumstances, etc. etc. not.'[16]

In the *Grammar* he comments on another likeness between the Illative Sense and *phronesis*. Just as the ability of the latter varies according to the personal experience and degree of development acquired in different fields of action, so to with the Illative Sense. It will be more effective in one domain of knowledge rather than another, according to our personal experience and training in that particular field.

His analogical comparison of the Illative Sense with Aristotle's *phronesis* is the most explicit and detailed appeal that he makes to the authority of another philosopher in order to corroborate his own position. I think that this serves to highlight the importance he wishes to give to this concept in his theory of knowledge.

After his comparison with *phronesis* he considers some others. He refers to the genius found in those who practice the fine arts that is not transferable from one artistic form to another: 'Genius is indissolubly united to one definite subject matter; a poet is not therefore a painter, or an architect a musical composer.'[17] This phenomenon also occurs with regard to different skills. In a parallel way the effectiveness of the Illative Sense found in different people with respect to the various fields of knowledge will vary according to their individual experience and expertise.

He ends his discussion on the nature of the Illative Sense in the *Grammar* with a brief summary of his conclusions. First, 'as viewed in itself' as an ability of the intellect, the Illative Sense has the characteristic of being 'the same in all concrete matter, though employed in them in different measures'. It forms part of the general operation of our intellect and is constantly in action. It is 'the more subtle and elastic logic of thought', rather than 'the logic of language', that sanctions our Assent. Its second characteristic is that it becomes more developed and accurate in some 'department of thought' rather than in others, according to our personal experience and training in that particular area of knowledge. The third is that 'it proceeds, always in the same way, by a method of reasoning, which ... is the elementary principle of mathematical calculus of modern times, which has so wonderfully extended the limits of abstract science'. This 'method of reasoning' is of course Informal Inference. The final characteristic that he mentions refers to our knowledge of individual reality, 'concrete reasonings'. He says there is no 'ultimate test of truth and error in our inferences besides the trustworthiness of the Illative Sense that gives them its sanction'.[18] To avoid any misunderstanding it is worth bearing in mind this constant emphasis that he gives in the *Grammar* to our reaching knowledge of individual reality. In the opening paragraphs of his chapter on the Illative Sense he repeats that this is his objective: 'My aim is of a practical character, ... I would confine myself to the truth of things, and the mind's certitude of that truth.'[19]

The more we try to know contingent reality with accuracy the greater the importance of the Illative Sense. For instance, it is not difficult to understand how crucial it becomes in determining an accurate forecast of the weather, where there are so many contingent factors to be taken into account. It also follows that in such fields of knowledge Informal rather than Formal Inference will be necessary.

Range

Having described the nature of the Illative Sense in his *Grammar* Newman then considers what he calls its 'range'. By this he means the function of the Illative Sense with regard to the different operations of the intellect. After reiterating the value of Formal Inference and reminds us that:

The mind itself is more versatile and vigorous than any of its works, of which language is one, and it is only under its penetrating and subtle action that the margin disappears, which I have described as intervening between verbal argumentation and conclusions in the concrete. It determines what science cannot determine, the limit of converging probabilities and the reasons sufficient for a proof.[20]

He identifies the Illative Sense with 'the reasoning faculty, as exercised by gifted, or by educated or otherwise well-prepared minds' and concludes that it 'has its function in the beginning, middle, and end of all verbal discussion and inquiry, and in every step of the process'.[21] In other words, the Illative Sense is present 'upon the whole course of thought from antecedents to consequents, with a minute diligence and unwearied presence'. It plays a part in the discovery of self-evident truths and premises with which all Inferences must rely. It is operative throughout all the reasoning processes and finally, its most evident role, is that of sanctioning Assent to our conclusions.

Since he has already considered its latter function he proceeds to 'illustrate its presence and action in relation to the elementary premises, and, again to the conduct of an argument'.[22] He begins by considering its role regarding our Inferences using an example taken from the field of historical investigation. The case involves five historians, each having the same evidence available to them, 'on the subject of the state of Greece and Rome during the pre-historic period'. He describes how their different treatment of the evidence and the arguments that they use brings them, not only to different conclusions, but even to apparently conflicting ones. This is not due to any particular fault in their reasoning, but rather because of the complexity of the topic combined with their own personal approach to the subject and use of inferences. He observes how they finally resort to criticizing each other, and concludes: 'Men become personal when logic fails; it is their mode of appealing to their own primary elements of thought, and their own illative sense against the principles and the judgment of another.'[23] He suggests that in controversies of this kind scholars ultimately have to rely on their own Illative Sense, and since this is unique to each individual it can lead them to very different conclusions.

After discussing another instance taken from historical

research he turns his attention to the role of the Illative Sense with respect to the 'first principles' involved in our reasoning. He says that 'the particular aspect under which we view a subject' can determine the course and conclusions of our Inferences. His first example of this type of general principle is based on the aspect 'under which we view the physical world'. For instance, whether we see it as 'a system of final causes, or, on the other hand, of initial or effective causes'.[24] He suggests that the success of Bacon as a scientist was partly due to his determination to consider reality in terms of 'effective causes'. By using this general principle 'He saw what others before him might have seen in what they saw, but who did not see as he saw it.' He concludes that our personal approach to reality, the particular aspect through which we view it, colours our reasoning to such a degree that it can even lead us to 'differ so widely from each other in religious and moral perceptions'.

Newman then considers the part played by the Illative Sense with regard to 'the implicit assumption of definite propositions in the first start of a course of reasoning, and the arbitrary exclusion of others'. Our Inferences must commence with true premises if they are to arrive at valid conclusions. Such premises consist of self-evident truths or first principles that are necessarily in the form of assumptions with respect to our Inferences. On the one hand, 'We have no right in argument to make any assumption we please.' However, he rejects the scepticism that presumes the 'general proposition that we have no right in philosophy to make any assumption whatever, and that we ought to begin with a universal doubt'. As we have seen, Newman's realism does not entertain any epistemological problem regarding the intellect's ability to know reality. Consequently, the intellect should be ever open to the possibility of new truths rather than adopting some form of methodical doubt. He affirms that this 'seems the true way of learning', and continues:

In that case we soon discover and discard what is contradictory to itself; and error having always some portion of truth in it, and the truth having a reality which error has not, we may expect, that when there is an honest purpose and fair talents, we shall somehow make our way forward, the error falling off from the mind, and the truth developing and occupying it.[25]

He proposes several examples of the acceptance of premises in reasoning that are taken from the domain of religious truth. Two of them deal with what he considers to be false premises leading to erroneous conclusions. For example, a religious system based on the assumption 'that Scripture is the Rule of Faith'. In another he touches on one of the major issues of his day, namely, as to whether the state should be exclusively secular in its approach to government, or based on some Christian principles. He concludes that such a debate ultimately becomes a 'conflict of first principles or assumptions'. He considers that any premise for our reasoning is the result of 'an act of the Illative Sense'. It may be erroneous due to 'acting on mistaken elements of thought'.

Newman also considers the role of the Illative Sense with respect to our Inferences, and in particular with 'antecedent reasons'. With this expression he refers to the converging probabilities involved in Informal Inference. He cautions against attributing to them a necessity that they may not have. For instance, our knowledge of the reputation of Alexander the Great for heroism might constitute an antecedent reason for rejecting a particular accusation against him of cowardice: 'antecedent reasoning, when negative is safe'. Nevertheless, this does not provide us with a guarantee that the whole life of Alexander was heroic. He concludes that: 'Facts cannot be proved by presumptions.'

Referring to natural science he remarks that the 'system of laws, by which physical nature is governed, makes it antecedently improbable that an exception should occur in it' is acceptable. However, this does not necessarily exclude that an exception may occur at some time. He dwells on this conclusion in the context of 'the controversy about the Plurality of worlds', which he suggests 'has been considered, on purely antecedent grounds'. He comments that the existence of intelligent beings on one planet is sometimes considered as a necessary reason to posit the existence of other such intelligent beings in the universe. His chapter on the Illative Sense ends with the conclusion: 'And in all these delicate questions there is constant call for the exercise of the Illative Sense.'[26]

Thus Newman proposes that the Illative Sense is a 'virtue', a 'power of judging' of the intellect in general. It is that aspect of the virtue of prudence that has as its specific objective the acquisition of truth. In this respect it may be referred to as an intellectual habit or virtue. As such it can be educated and developed in different fields of knowledge. Consequently, it exists in varying degrees of perfection in each individual according to their personal experience and training.

In the course of time the intellect makes more and more Assents within a particular domain of knowledge. Subsequent experience shows some of them to be true. Thus we acquire knowledge, and the mind gradually learns how to make more correct Assents in that field. The Illative Sense develops in that particular sphere of knowledge and, being an active habit of the intellect, has a part to play in all its operations. Although it is in the context of Informal Inference that its role is more clearly discernible, it is also present in both Formal and Natural Inference.

I think that Newman's view of Illative Sense agrees basically with the tradition of Aquinas that would envisage it as the active intellectual habit of science. Here I consider science in its broadest possible sense, as embracing all areas of knowledge, whether with regard to speculative truth or individual reality. It is that aspect of prudence which enables us to Assent to truth, and in particular with respect to concrete reality.[27]

A Misunderstanding

It has been insinuated by some authors that Newman invents the Illative Sense to bridge the logical gap, which he himself had created, between the conditional nature of the conclusions of our Inferences and that of the unconditional characteristic of our Assents.[28] That is to say, it is a convenient solution to solve a self-inflicted problem. Since he affirms that all conclusions of

Inferences contain an element of probability when referring to individual reality, he therefore has to find a way to justify his assertion that our Assent can reach certitude.

Even Copleston, at one point in his appraisal of Informal Inference, gives the impression of ambiguity:

> But it can still be objected against Newman that no definite rule can be given for determining when the truth of a certain conclusion is the only possible rational explanation of a given convergence. Hence though we may be perfectly justified in assuming the truth of the conclusion for all practical purposes, an unconditional or unqualified assent is unjustified.[29]

As has already been mentioned, this is precisely the point Newman is trying to make. There is no external rule that we can apply. It is only the human intellect that possesses the ability inherent in its nature, an acquired habit, to assess all the rational evidence and to make the appropriate Assent. Just a few lines later Copleston redeems himself by saying that: 'The convergence of probabilities amounts to conclusive proof. This is the illative sense.'

In the *Grammar* Newman seems to have anticipated this possible misunderstanding regarding the Illative Sense when he says:

> There is no ultimate test of truth besides the testimony borne to truth by the mind itself, and that this phenomenon, perplexing as we may find it, is a normal and inevitable characteristic of the mental constitution of a being like man on a stage such as the world.[30]

Some may find it 'perplexing' because they have not fully appreciated the depth of Newman's thought. There is no gap to bridge since the whole intellectual process takes place within the unity of the individual mind. As Collins points out, the Illative Sense is not a separate entity or faculty operating between our Inferences and Assents.[31] Apprehension, Inference and Assent designate distinct operations of the one intellect. The Illative

Sense, however, is that general active habit of the same intellect that enables us to judge the reasonableness of assenting to the truth of a particular conclusion.

As noticed by Ker, it was when he wrote the *Grammar* that Newman began to use the term Illative Sense.[32] However, as happened with some of his other concepts, it had been developing in his mind over a period of many years before coming to its definitive formulation in the *Grammar*.

Rudimentary elements of this concept are already present in some of his *University Sermons*, especially in the context of what he then called 'Implicit Reason', an idea which will eventually become Informal and Natural Inference. When referring to the personal nature of our reasoning he suggests that it is under the control of some 'inward faculty'.[33] It is not difficult to understand this notion in terms of the Illative Sense. Just a few years later, in his *Development of Christian Doctrine*, he speaks of the reasoning process being 'under the scrutiny and sanction of a prudent judgment'.[34] In one of his lectures published in his *Idea of a University* he refers to the Illative Sense in all but name. What he says suggests the development of this concept. After lamenting that there does not appear to be an appropriate word in English to refer to it, he comments:

> In default of a recognized term, I have called the perfection or virtue of the intellect by the name of philosophy, philosophical knowledge, enlargement of mind, or illumination; ... but, whatever name we bestow on it, it is ... the business of a University to make this intellectual culture its direct scope, or to employ itself in the education of the intellect.[35]

Some of his private notes also show how this concept, as yet without a specific name, was evolving in his mind:

> This Prudentia is partly a natural endowment common to all, or a special gift to certain persons, partly the result of experience; and it varies in its worth and preciousness, and its rarity, with the subject matter on which it is employed.[36]

In an entry of 1865 in his *Philosophical Notebook* he already compares it to Aristotle's *phronesis*, and refers to it as our ability 'in determining *when* we ought to be certain'.[37]

This brief historical parenthesis on the development of the Illative Sense in Newman's writings shows clearly, if any evidence were necessary, that it was not some last minute invention to fill a supposed gap between Inference and Assent.

In the opening paragraph of chapter three, when I began to examine Newman's theory of knowledge, I stated that I intended to follow his own criteria for such an appraisal. I have analysed his understanding of the cognitive process in terms of the different operations of the intellect that he refers to as Apprehension, Assent and Inference. I have considered in the first half of the present chapter the overall governing virtue of the intellect that he calls the Illative Sense. At the same time, throughout my analysis, I have endeavoured to indicate and answer some of the more serious objections that might be brought against his philosophical view and his approach to knowledge.

Education

There are some other interesting aspects of his gnoseology that, although they are touched on in the *Grammar*, are not dealt with in a systematic way. They can be adequately complemented, however, from what is found in the other sources of Newman's philosophy, especially from his *Idea of a University*.

Referring to the Illative Sense in the *Grammar* he explains that a human is 'a being of progress with relation to his perfection and characteristic good ... but man begins with nothing realized (to use the word), and he has to make capital for himself by the exercise of those faculties which are his natural inheritance'. 'Progress is carried out', he continues, 'by means of the acquisition of knowledge, of which inference and assent are the immediate instruments.'[38]

This progress in terms of knowledge can be viewed from two perspectives. It can be seen in terms of the development and increase of our personal circle of knowledge in the sense of education. On the other hand, it can be viewed as the general advance of mankind in terms of scientific knowledge.

Growth and development is a recurring theme in his writings.[39] The human mind acquires more knowledge by continually being disposed towards assenting to propositions that come before the intellect for its scrutiny. In his book, *On the Development of Christian Doctrine,* he states:

> It is the characteristic of our minds to be ever engaged in passing judgement on the things which come before us. No sooner do we apprehend than we judge: we allow nothing to stand by itself: we compare, contrast, abstract, generalize, connect, adjust, classify: and we view all our knowledge in the associations with which these processes have invested it.[40]

A few pages later he gives a synthesis of his approach to development in the following sentence: 'In a higher world it is otherwise, but here below to live is to change, and to be perfect is to have changed often.'[41]

Personal effort is needed if an individual is to progress 'in the circle of his knowledge'.[42] In his *Grammar* he says:

> Nor is this progress mechanical, nor is it of necessity; it is committed to the personal efforts of each individual of the species; each of us has the prerogative of completing his inchoate and rudimental nature, and of developing his own perfection out of the living elements with which his mind began to be.[43]

He continues by saying that the intellect needs a specific training and development since 'Progress is a living growth, not a mechanism; and its instruments are mental actions, not the formulas and contrivances of language.' This process, during the first years of our life, 'is almost passive in the acquisition of knowledge'.[44] However, education implies the training of the intellect itself if it is to be effective in its quest for truth:

The intellect admits of an education; man is a being of progress; he has to learn how to fulfil his end, and to be what facts show that he is intended to be. His mind is in the first instance in disorder, and runs wild; his faculties have their rudimental and inchoate state, and are gradually carried on by practice and experience to their perfection.[45]

As we have already seen, this means beginning with the right disposition towards reality. We must accept reality as we find it, and not as we might wish or imagine it to be. Similarly, to take the nature of our intellect as it is, with its ability to come to the knowledge of reality if we use it correctly.

Newman gives special emphasis to the personal possession of self-evident truths and first principles of science in the different fields of knowledge, since they will constitute the premises for our inferences.[46] Experience and time are needed in order to increase our knowledge in any particular area. An assiduous contemplation of reality by the intellect is essential if the self-evident truths and the basic principles necessary for any true personal advance in knowledge is to be achieved.[47]

It is in this context that he uses the word realization.[48] As we have seen, to realize implies the acquisition of a more profound ontological appreciation of reality, as opposed to the possession of abstract notions about it. For instance, he uses this idea to clarify his distinction between Notional and Real Apprehension:

To apprehend notionally is to have breadth of mind, but to be shallow; to apprehend really is to be deep, but to be narrow-minded. ... However, real apprehension has the precedence, as being the scope and end and the test of notional; and the fuller is the mind's hold upon things or what it considers such, the more fertile is it in its aspect of them, and the more practical in its definitions.[49]

Newman does not provide us with a precise definition of realization. Nonetheless, it is clear that it involves a more intensive reflection, a profound intellectual contemplation, of some specific reality. It may need particular personal experience, or take a considerable period of time, in order for our knowledge of an individual reality to reach a certain ontological fullness. It implies that we bring all our potencies of knowing to bear on the reality in question, and not just our ability to reason abstractly. This will usually involve all our senses, both external and internal, together with all the potentialities of our intellect. That is to say, in the terminology of Aquinas, to use all our powers of knowing, both of individual beings (*ratio particularis*), and of their essences (*ratio universalis*). This of course will also include our powers of inference and of our knowledge of all its relationships with regard to other realities; our Illative Sense. I think that there are various elements of Newman's concept of realization present in the thought of Aquinas.[50]

Realization involves a more personal, living relationship of the knowing subject to the apprehended object. The constant endeavour to realize will act as a safeguard to the dangers of an idealized or superficial way of thinking, of confusing our thinking with knowing.

One example that can illustrate this concept is to consider the difference between a child's knowledge of death, before, and then after, his first experience of seeing a corpse. Such a child may have some Notional Assents, all of them true, regarding the phenomenon of human death. However, these Assents can become vividly real when he encounters the dead body of his beloved grandfather who has unexpectedly died. His original Notional Assents become Real Assents in the measure that he now begins to appreciate the individual reality of death.

As we have seen, in order to achieve a personal advance in a particular branch of knowledge we need to acquire the relevant self-evident truths and first principles. This usually implies that each individual is limited to having a truly profound knowledge in only a certain number of fields. Newman says: 'On only few subjects have any of us the opportunity of realizing in our minds what we speak and hear about.'[51]

The Illative Sense, being part of the virtue of prudence, is an active quality of the mind. It develops in parallel with our personal experience of reality and continually expanding sphere of knowledge. Since each specific domain of knowledge possesses its own self-evident truths and valid assumptions, so a corresponding development of the Illative Sense is needed in this same area.[52] Newman, before quoting Aristotle in support of his own conviction, affirms 'that a special preparation of mind is required for each separate department of inquiry'.[53] This becomes even more essential in those areas of research that deal directly with contingent matter, such as the positive and empirical sciences. This is due to the fact that in these areas of knowledge our personal experience of the reality in question and our use of Informal Inference are more critical, if we wish to advance accurately in knowledge.[54]

A well-developed Illative Sense in one area is no guarantee that it will function with equal accuracy in other spheres of knowledge: 'Few there are, ... who are good reasoners on all subject-matters. Two men, who reason well each in his own province of thought, may, one or both of them, fail and pronounce opposite judgments on a question belonging to some third province.'[55] It is notorious, for example, how on occasions a well-known scientist will make a pronouncement on some topic outside his field of knowledge and make a fool of himself.[56] Newman remarks: 'So is it with Ratiocination; and as we should betake ourselves to Newton for physical, not for theological conclusions, and to Wellington for his military experience, not for statesmanship, so the maxim holds good generally, "Cuique in arte sua credendum est".'[57]

Another way of advancing our circle of knowledge is to accept the truths already gained by others who are true experts in their field. Newman is true to his own convictions by quoting Aristotle on occasions to lend authority to his own conclusions.[58] For example, when precisely referring to this point and after citing Aristotle, he affirms: 'Instead of trusting logical science, we must trust persons, namely, those who by long acquaintance with their subject have a right to judge.'[59] It is interesting to note that in his discussion of this same topic Aquinas makes use of exactly the same quotation from Aristotle to support his view.[60] Accepting the conclusions of experts applies particularly with respect to those areas of knowledge where Formal Inference is unable to provide suitable explanations. In other words, where there is greater necessity of having attained the self-evident truths and a developed Illative Sense in that particular field.

To increase our circle of knowledge demands a training of the intellect itself to enable it to seek truth in a more effective way. Earlier in this chapter, with respect to the Illative Sense, I mentioned that in his *Idea of a University* he refers to this integral formation of the intellect using several different expressions. The one he tends to use more frequently is 'enlargement of mind'.[61] He explains this concept in the following way:

> Truth of whatever kind is the proper object of the intellect; its cultivation then lies in fitting it to apprehend and contemplate truth. ... We know, not by a direct and simple vision, ... but, ... by a mental process, by going round an object, by the comparison, the combination, the mutual correction, the continual adaptation, of many partial notions, by the employment, concentration, and joint action of many faculties and exercises of mind. Such a union and concert of the intellectual powers, ... is necessarily a matter of training. ... it is not mere application, however exemplary, which introduces the mind to truth, nor the reading many books, nor the getting up many subjects, nor the witnessing many experiments, nor the attending many lectures. ... a man may have done it all, yet be lingering in the vestibule of knowledge: – he may not realize what his mouth utters; he may not see with his mental eye what confronts him; he may have no grasp of things as they are; or at least he may have no power at all of advancing one step forward of himself, in consequence of what he has already acquired, ... if I may use the phrase, of building up ideas. Such a power is the result of a scientific formation of mind; it is an acquired faculty of judgment, of clear sightedness, of sagacity, of wisdom, of philosophical reach of mind, and of intellectual self-possession and repose, – qualities which do not come of mere acquirement. ... the eye of the mind, of which the object is truth, is the work of discipline and habit.[62]

For Newman this is the purpose of a university education and forms the central thesis of his *Idea of a University*: 'When the intellect has once been properly trained and formed ... it will be a faculty of entering with comparative ease into any subject of thought, and of taking up with aptitude any science or profession.'[63]

This education of the intellect that produces a genuine philosophical spirit within the individual affects his whole personality.[64] Such a view seems to agree with that of Aquinas, namely, that the authentic increase in a person's knowledge brings with it a true enrichment of being.

It is easy to appreciate the coherence between Newman's gnoseology and his understanding of education. We find the same insistence on the importance of acquiring self-evident truths and first principles in the various areas of knowledge. Hence the intellect is able to build the foundation of a coherent system on which to relate and incorporate new truths. Specific importance is given to Real Apprehension and Real Assent. Education must not remain just at the level of a mere imparting of information, but rather on leading the student into acquiring the most profound realization of truths. It entails teaching to apprehend, to reason and to realize the truths of reality. In other words, a general development of the Illative Sense is necessary together with any specific training in a particular field of knowledge.

Science

The second perspective of progress in knowledge is that of its increase considered as the common patrimony of mankind. Just as individuals have the ability of reaching certitude and increasing their 'circle of knowledge' so to can society at large. Referring to Assent Newman tells us:

This is the process by which knowledge accumulates and is stored up both in the individual and in the world. It has sometimes been remarked, when men have boasted of the knowledge of modern times, that no wonder we see more than the ancients, because we are mounted upon their shoulders. The conclusions of one generation are the truths of the next. We are able, it is our duty, deliberately to take things for granted which our forefathers had a duty to doubt about; and unless we summarily put down disputation on points which have been already proved and ruled, we shall waste our time, and make no advances.[65]

This general advance in terms of scientific knowledge is the consequence of the combined efforts of many individuals over a period of time:

There are no short cuts to knowledge; nor does the road to it always lie in the direction in which it terminates, nor are we able to see the end on starting. . . . Moreover, it is not often the fortune of any one man to live through an investigation; the process is one of not only many stages, but of many minds. What one begins another finishes; and a true conclusion is at length worked out by the co-operation of independent schools and the perseverance of successive generations.[66]

When new advances in science are dependent on self-evident truths that are accepted by many, and supported by irrefutable Formal Inferences, then the communication and widespread acceptance of them is relatively straightforward. Newman comments: 'All of us have the power of abstraction, and can be taught either to make or to enter into the same abstractions; and thus to co-operate in the establishment of a common measure between mind and mind.'[67] Notional Apprehension and Notional Assent are essential for progress in our common knowledge; 'to apprehend notionally is to have breadth of mind', and referring to knowledge, he says that this is 'the principle of its advancement. Without the apprehension of notions we should for ever pace round one small circle of knowledge'.[68]

Our Notional Assents, given their universal nature, provide the premises for our Formal Inferences, the uses of which 'are manifold':

It is the great principle of order in thinking; it reduces a chaos into harmony; it catalogues the accumulations of knowledge; it maps out for us the relations of its separate departments; it puts us in the way to correct its own mistakes. It enables the independent intellects of many, acting and re-acting on each other, to bring their collective force to bear upon one and the same subject-matter, or the same question. ... Though it does not itself discover the unknown, it is one principal way by which discoveries are made. [69]

Thus Formal Inference plays a central role in the advancement of science. Not just as used by the individual, but as an instrument for the development and increase of knowledge common to all mankind. Science is the ordered knowledge of reality that seeks to know and understand the causes of physical reality. It searches for those more universal and necessary aspects of reality within the particular and contingent. Formal Inference is not only a useful tool for this task, but also becomes a means for its universal communication. It facilitates the acknowledgement of the validity of scientific conclusions, and is also the great vehicle for their communication. Newman, referring to such conclusions, says:

Thus they serve to transfer our knowledge from the custody of memory to the surer and more abiding protection of philosophy, thereby providing both for its spread and its advance: – for, inasmuch as sciences are forms of knowledge, they enable the intellect to master and increase it; and, inasmuch as they are instruments, to communicate it readily to others. [70]

Scientific knowledge in the public domain is usually accompanied by Formal Inferences. At least to the extent that Formal Inferences support its veracity with appropriate explanations. However, the apparent absence or weakness of such explanations for some scientific theory should not lead us to immediately conclude that it must be erroneous. Such a theory may already be, in the minds of many scientists, a certitude based on Informal or Natural Inference. Nonetheless, we may have the situation that no Formal Inferences sufficient to demonstrate this theory have been forthcoming as yet. As we have seen, Newman stresses that we should have respect for the conclusions of experts in their own specific field of knowledge. He cites the example of Newton who, on occasions, had difficulty in proving his scientific discoveries. He himself was certain but was unable, in the first instance, to provide adequate Formal Inferences to demonstrate them to others. Newman comments that:

> He was obliged to invent a calculus in order to prove them, ... It was his prudentia which made them credible to him, presenting to him a proof of their credibility, which he could not communicate to another. So he went about to invent a scientific proof of their truth.[71]

If a science is of an abstract or theoretical nature then we are entitled to ask for the corresponding Formal Inferences to support their conclusions as a warrant for claiming our acceptance.[72] On the other hand, with those sciences that we refer to as positive or empirical, because they deal more directly with reality as contingent and individual, we need to modify our approach. That is to say, with regard to those sciences that rely more on Informal rather than Formal Inference, and requiring a well developed Illative Sense in that particular sphere. We have already seen such an example in the *Grammar* where Newman concludes: 'Men become personal when logic fails; it is their mode of appealing to their own primary elements of thought, and their own illative sense, against the principles and the judgment of another.'[73] This phenomenon is due to the nature of the intellect since the Illative Sense of each individual 'supplies no common measure between mind and mind, as being nothing else than a personal gift or acquisition'.[74]

Such a situation should not give rise to scepticism. With respect to the progress of such sciences we need to carefully consider the particular role played by the intellect. We should be aware that, as individuals, we may differ in our possession of the specific self-evident truths and first principles that they involve.

Consequently, if we start from different premises then the conclusions of our Inferences will vary. Furthermore, since in these sciences we are more likely to rely on Informal Inference, then it is quite probable that there will also be a difference in the development of the Illative Sense. Therefore, it should not come as any surprise that in these cases 'there is no common measure of minds'.[75]

When we try to deepen our knowledge of concrete, contingent reality, Informal Inference and the Illative Sense take on fundamental roles. They provide us with the way forward in our research, but there is a price to pay. Since our conclusions seem to defy adequate expression in terms of Formal Inferences they can appear to be less scientific. In order to contribute to the universal increase of knowledge in such a situation it is not just a question of Formal Inferences, but also that of communicating our personal experience of the realities involved. Communication, in its widest possible sense, becomes all important if we wish others to benefit from the increase in knowledge achieved by any one individual. Real Apprehension and Real Assents, due to their more personal nature, are difficult to communicate.[76] In these cases, to pass on our experience and conclusions, it will be necessary to provide detailed descriptions and carefully chosen illustrations in order to lead others towards appreciating the same Real Apprehensions, and to make the same Real Assents. In this way they will be in a better position to consider the reasonableness of our conclusions derived from Informal Inference:

It will be our wisdom to avail ourselves of language, as far as it will go, but to aim mainly by means of it to stimulate, in those to whom we address ourselves, a mode of thinking and trains of thought similar to our own, leading them on by their own independent action, not by any syllogistic compulsion.[77]

In those sciences whose conclusions are not easily demonstrated by means of Formal Inferences, where we are compelled to rely more on the findings of individual scientists, we must also take into account certain personal factors. For instance, the intellectual integrity of the scientists involved. With respect to a specific science appropriate criteria needs to be formulated that makes it possible to judge when it is truly reasonable to accept the findings of others. That is to say, specific criteria that will enable us to judge the credibility of their conclusions. These would include factors such as, whether a scientist possesses sufficient experience of the realities involved, has acquired the necessary self-evident truths and valid assumptions, or whether he has a well developed Illative Sense in that particular branch of knowledge. On this point Newman appeals to Aristotle for support:

> A well-educated man will expect exactness in every class of subject according as the nature of the thing admits; for it is much the same mistake to put up with a mathematician using probabilities, and to require demonstration of an orator. Each man judges skilfully in those things about which he is well-informed; it is of these that he is a good judge; viz. he, in each subject-matter, is a judge, who is well-educated in that subject-matter, and he is in an absolute sense a judge, who is in all of them well-educated.[78]

Using criteria such as these we will be in a better position to assess whether or not the conclusions of the individual scientists are truly reasonable, and therefore credible. Such a judgement will be made easier 'if the principles or facts assumed have a large following'.[79]

To become an expert in any field demands the education and development of our Illative Sense in that particular sphere of knowledge. However, such specialization should respect the overall coherence of truth and our universal knowledge of reality. To facilitate progress, according to Newman, there should be an interaction among the different sciences. The truths of any individual science should be shown as coherent with that of others, since together they all form part of our knowledge of the one reality. Referring to this unity and harmony of the sciences he remarks: 'Viewed altogether, they approximate to a representation or subjective reflection of the objective truth, as nearly as is possible to the human mind, which advances towards the accurate apprehension of that object.'[80]

Considered in this way the different sciences are seen as being both complementary and mutually corrective. Since each deals with a different aspect of the same reality hence there should not be any contradiction between the conclusions of the one and the other: 'As regards the whole circle of sciences, one corrects another for purposes of fact, and one without the other cannot dogmatize, except hypothetically and upon its own abstract principles.'[81] If research in a particular field does not take into account the conclusions of other related sciences then this mutually corrective function may be lost, and the risk of error will increase: 'The systematic omission of any one science from the catalogue prejudices the accuracy and completeness of our knowledge altogether, and that, in proportion to its importance.'[82]

A true awareness of this harmony among the sciences, since they all seek the understanding of the same reality, opens up the possibility of a positive cross-fertilization of ideas among them for their mutual benefit: 'The Sciences, into which our knowledge may be said to be cast, have multiplied bearings one on another, and an internal sympathy, and admit, or rather demand, comparison and adjustment. They complete, correct, balance each other.'[83] According to Newman the achievement of this objective is the precise role of the university as an educational and research institution. This is one of the principal conclusions of his book, *The Idea of a University*.[84]

Notes

1. Ward, vol. II, p. 246; cf. Norris, pp. 36–7, 44, 205–6.
2. Harrold, 'Introduction', in *GA* (1947), p. xvii.
3. *LD* XXIV, p. 275.
4. *GA*, p. 222 (344).
5. *GA*, p. 221 (342).
6. *GA*, pp. 227–8 (353).
7. *GA*, p. 233 (361).
8. Cf. Walgrave, *Newman. Le développement du dogme*, reference is to the English translation, pp. 106–12; Reid, essay VI, chapter 2, pp. 421–2.

9. Cf. Ker, 'Introduction', in *GA* (1985), pp. lxv–lxvi.
10. *GA*, p. 225 (349); cf. *Dev*, p. 40; *Diff* II, pp. 78–9.
11. *GA*, p. 226 (350).
12. *GA*, pp. 227–8 (353).
13. Cf. Aristotle, *Nicomachean Ethics*, book VI, v–xiii.
14. *GA*, p. 228 (354) footnote 1.
15. *GA*, p. 232 (360).
16. *LD* XXIX, p. 115; cf. *LD* XXIV, p. 105; *LD* XXV, p. 280; *LD* XXVI, pp. 40–1; *LD* XXIX, p. 119; *Phil N* II, p. 195.
17. *GA*, p. 230 (358).
18. *GA*, p. 231 (359).
19. *GA*, pp. 222–3 (344).
20. *GA*, p. 232 (360).
21. *GA*, p. 233 (361).
22. *GA*, p. 234 (363).
23. *GA*, p. 238 (369).
24. *GA*, p. 239 (372).
25. *GA*, p. 243 (377).
26. *GA*, p. 247 (383).
27. Cf. Aquinas, *Summa Theologiae* I–II, q. 57, a. 2; ibid., I–II, q. 58, a. 3; ibid., II–II, q. 47, a. 3, *corpus*, also ad 1 and ad 3; ibid., II–II, q. 49, a. 2 ad 1 and ad 3, also a. 5 ad 2.
28. Cf. Pailin, pp. 168, 173; O'Donoghue, p. 245.
29. Copleston, vol. VIII, p. 522.
30. *GA*, p. 226 (350).
31. Cf. Collins, pp. 22, 44.
32. Cf. Ker, 'Introduction', in *GA* (1985), pp. xxiii, xxx, xxxii.
33. *US*, p. 257; cf. ibid., pp. 66, 211–13, 277.
34. *Dev*, p. 327; cf. ibid., p. 115.
35. *Idea*, p. 125.
36. *TP* I, p. 24; cf. ibid., pp. 30, 36–8; *Phil N* II, p. 29.
37. *Phil N* II, p. 163.
38. *GA*, p. 225 (349); cf. ibid., p. 152 (233).
39. Cf. *Diff* II, pp. 78–9; *Apo*, pp. 109, 264.
40. *Dev*, p. 33.
41. *Dev*, p. 40.
42. *GA*, p. 112 (169); cf. ibid., pp. 29 (34), 115 (173); *Idea*, p. 73.
43. *GA*, p. 225 (349); cf. *US*, p. 253; *Idea*, pp. xvi–xvii, 474–5; *TP* I, p. 72.
44. *Idea*, p. 128; cf. ibid., p. 134.
45. *GA*, p. 152 (233).

46. Cf. *GA*, pp. 239–42 (372–5); *Idea*, pp. 139–42.
47. Cf. *GA*, pp. 266–7 (414–15); *TP* I, pp. 30, 74, 106–12; *Dev*, p. 190; *Phil N* II, p. 29.
48. Cf. *SE* II, p. 303.
49. *GA*, pp. 29–30 (34); cf. ibid., pp. 56–60 (77–84), 66 (93), 225 (348–9), *passim*; *PS* I, sermon 4; *PS* IV, sermon 6; *US*, pp. 320; 329–31; *Idea*, p. 152.
50. Cf. Aquinas, *Summa Theologiae* I, q. 85, a. 3 and a. 5.
51. *GA*, p. 29 (33).
52. Cf. *GA*, pp. 233 (361–2), 266–7 (414–15); *TP* I, p. 26.
53. *GA*, p. 266 (414).
54. Cf. *GA*, pp. 266–7 (414–15).
55. *GA*, p. 233 (362).
56. Cf. *GA*, pp. 218–20 (338–41); *Idea*, pp. xv–xvi, 76–8.
57. *GA*, p. 220 (341); cf. ibid., p. 266 (414); *Dev*, p. 83; *TP* I, pp. 22, 26–7, 74; *Idea*, p. 101.
58. Cf. *GA*, pp. 228–30 (353–7), 266–7 (414–15).
59. *GA*, p. 221 (342).
60. Cf. *Summa Theologiae* II–II, q. 49, a. 3; Aristotle, *Nicomachean Ethics*, book VI, xii, 6.
61. Cf. *Idea*, pp. 125, 133–4, 136, 137.
62. *Idea*, pp. 151–2; cf. ibid., pp. 125–6, 134, 136–7, 139–42, 502.
63. *Idea*, pp. xvii–xviii, cf. ibid., pp. xvi-xx, 113–14, 122–3, 124–5, 151–3, 165–6, 332, 495–502.
64. Cf. *Idea*, pp. 113–14, 139.
65. *GA*, p. 150 (229–30); cf. *PS* VII, p. 248.
66. *Idea*, pp. 474–5.
67. *GA*, p. 60 (83).
68. *GA*, p. 29 (34).
69. *GA*, pp. 185–6 (285); cf. *TP* I, pp. 93–4.
70. *Idea*, p. 46.
71. *TP* I, p. 25.
72. Cf. *GA*, pp. 265–6 (412–14).
73. *GA*, p. 238 (369).
74. *GA*, p. 233 (362).
75. *GA*, p. 266 (413).
76. Cf. *GA*, p. 60 (83–4).
77. *GA*, pp. 200–1 (309); cf. *TP* I, pp. 26–7.
78. *Nichomachean Ethics*, book I, iii, 4; *GA*, p. 266 (414); cf. *TP* I, p. 25.
79. *GA*, p. 83 (122).

80. *Idea*, p. 47; cf. ibid., p. 50.
81. *Idea*, p. 49.
82. *Idea*, p. 51.
83. *Idea*, p. 99.
84. Cf. *Idea*, pp. 101–2.

CHAPTER 7

THE FUTURE

The purpose of this final chapter is to evaluate Newman's contribution to the advance of philosophy, to speculate on its future influence, and to consider whether I have achieved my overall goal. That is to say, to show that he should be considered as one of the more notable philosophers of the nineteenth century and therefore merit a place in the history of philosophy.

It will be remembered that he never wrote a treatise on philosophy, and even judged his *Grammar* to be 'characterised by incompleteness and crudeness'. Thus it would be wholly unfair to criticize him for what might be deemed as omissions in his philosophical view. I share the opinion of Copleston who, at the end of his review of Newman's thought, concluded:

> Hence those who take an interest in his philosophical reflections tend to look on them as a source of stimulus and inspiration rather than as a rigid, systematic doctrine, which, of course, Newman himself never intended them to be. And in this case detailed criticism of particular points necessarily seems pedantic and appears, to those who value Newman's general approach, as more or less irrelevant.[1]

Both from his philosophical background, and from what we have seen in the course of this appraisal of his philosophical thought, his basic approach is that of Aristotle. This is reflected in the *Grammar*, for instance, by the fact that he adopts in broad terms, the three operations of the intellect as envisaged by Aristotle, namely, apprehension, judgement and reasoning. Sillem boldly proclaims that his philosophy is a 'metaphysics of being as known in experience'.[2] I would not go quite so far. However, based on the evidence that we find in his writings, I would propose that his philosophy is permeated with an implicit metaphysics of being. At first sight such an hypothesis might appear to be somewhat gratuitous. Nowhere do we find any discussion on the nature of being as such. Nevertheless, if we place the emphasis on implicit, then I think that such a theory is reasonable. The various parallels that I have already been able to draw between the conclusions of Newman and those of Aquinas bear witness to its feasibility. It is arguable that such similarities would not occur unless Newman's view, like that of Aquinas, was based on a metaphysics of being. Or, put in positive terms, if both philosophies are founded on a metaphysics of being then it is perfectly logical to expect that at least some of their conclusions would coincide.

Possibly one of the most fundamental parallels which reveals this underlying approach is that they both acknowledge the existence of reality to be self-evident, and that the human intellect, from its very nature, is able to know this reality. Things both exist in reality and can be known by us. There is a true relationship between beings in reality and that other form of being, that of being known. If something is known, then not only does that something have its own being, but it also has a certain kind of being in the knowing subject. Gilson affirms that such a foundation for the science of knowledge, which was also that of Aquinas, is only possible if derived from a metaphysics of being: 'Starting from being, one can have knowledge; on the contrary, if one decides to start from the act of cognition of the knowing subject considered as an absolute point of departure, one will never get out of it.'[3]

What are the elements of Newman's 'philosophical reflections' that Copleston refers to as providing 'a source of stimulus and inspiration'? We might rephrase this question in the following way: What are his major contributions to contemporary philosophy? There is no doubt that deciding on his most significant insights is made all the more challenging given his rather unsystematic approach. I give my answer under three headings: *The Unity of Man*, *Informal Inference* and *The Illative Sense*.

The Unity of Man

An essential characteristic of Newman's gnoseology, as we have seen, is that it is person-centred: 'Every one who reasons, is his own centre.' All expressions of truth, in whatever form they take, are the consequence of the knowledge possessed by the one individual or the many. Knowledge is always that as held by a person, irrespective of whether it can be expressed adequately or communicated to others. The cognitive process takes place in the mind of the person; only the individual can possess knowledge and certitude. This is a recurring theme in his writings.[4]

The personalism associated with his thought has nothing to do with any form of subjectivism or immanentism. Such positions would clearly contradict his realism. Reality is both the source and objective of all knowing: 'Our being, with its faculties, mind and body, is a fact not admitting of question, all things being of necessity referred to it, not it to other things.'[5] His personalism expresses the fact that knowledge, in the strict philosophical sense, can only belong to the person. Sillem and Norris also give importance to this aspect of Newman's approach to knowledge.[6] It is a direct consequence of his profound appreciation for the unity of man in all his actions. This fundamental element of his anthropology is found implicitly throughout his writings.

Sometimes he expresses this integral unity of the human being with considerable force. One such example is found among comments he makes on the *Logic* of Mill who, at one point, seems to imply that there exists a certain dichotomy between mind and body. Newman exclaims:

I can't quite stomach the idea, as expressing a *fact*, that I have no consciousness of *Self*, as such, as distinct from a bundle of sensations. Bishop Butler speaks of consciousness as indivisible and one – this is my idea of man – of no unity have we practically experience, but of self.[7]

In his *Apologia*, talking of his own personal development in terms of religious faith, he says:

> I had a great dislike of paper logic. For myself, it was not logic that carried me on; as well might one say that the quicksilver in the barometer changes the weather. It is the concrete being that reasons; pass a number of years, and I find my mind in a new place; how? The whole man moves; paper logic is but the record of it.[8]

He touches of this idea several times in his *Grammar*: 'It is the mind that reasons, and that controls its own reasonings, not any technical apparatus of words and propositions.'[9] He often expresses his aversion to any narrow rationalistic tendency towards knowing: 'After all, man is *not* a reasoning animal; he is a seeing, feeling, contemplating, acting animal. He is influenced by what is direct and precise.'[10] With such a statement he is not of course suggesting that we are not endowed with a spark of intelligence: 'We are conscious of the objects of external nature, and we reflect and act upon them, and this consciousness, reflection, and action we call our own rationality.'[11] He is trying to stress the personal freedom and responsibility involved in our quest for truth, in contrast with a slavish acceptance of some externally imposed logic:

> We have arrived at these conclusions – not *ex opere operato*, by a scientific necessity independent of ourselves, – but by the action of our own minds, by our own individual perception of the truth in question, under a sense of duty to these conclusions and with an intellectual conscientiousness.[12]

It is the person who knows and acts: 'Of course, for convenience, we speak of the mind as possessing faculties instead of saying that it acts in a certain way and on a definite subject-matter; but we must not turn a figure of speech into a fact.'[13]

It will be remembered that any form of methodical doubt in tackling philosophical questions is quite alien to Newman's thought. His approach, as Sillem also notices, is that of intellectual humility, to be ever open to the possibility of knowing reality.[14] The ability to know implies a dynamic interchange between the individual and reality, and between those who are able to communicate this knowledge to one another. Jaki, after referring to the *Grammar* as his 'finest philosophical work', comments that the essence of its argument is that:

Truth, natural and supernatural, can only be grasped through a dynamical approach to it, the very opposite to the reductionist or 'scientific' approach. In this age when philosophers are eager to barter their subject in order to appear 'scientific', the *Grammar of Assent* should appear particularly relevant.[15]

As a consequence of his appreciation of the integral unity of the human being Newman stresses the effect that moral factors can have on the operations of the intellect. The proverb he cites in the *Grammar* provides an apt summary of his view: 'A man convinced against his will, Is of the same opinion still.'[16] Some chapters later he explains:

That truth there is, and attainable it is, but that its rays stream in upon us through the medium of our moral as well as our intellectual being; and that in consequence that perception of its first principles which is natural to us is enfeebled, obstructed, perverted, by allurements of sense and the supremacy of self.[17]

A lack of intellectual honesty, or prejudice, can hinder our pursuit for truth in any particular field of knowledge. On the other hand, a sincere love for the truth will enhance the effectiveness of our intellect:

I would maintain that the fear of error is simply necessary to the genuine love of truth. No inquiry comes to good which is not conducted under a deep sense of responsibility, and of the issues depending upon its determination. Even the ordinary matters of life are an exercise of conscientiousness; and where conscience is, fear must be.[18]

Referring to his *Grammar* in a letter of 1871 he commented: 'My book is to show that a moral state of mind germinates good intellectual principles.'[19] The importance that he gives to the genuine love for the truth and moral rectitude in our quest for knowledge constitutes another similarity with the thought of Aquinas.[20]

We have seen how his distinctions between Real and Notional, with respect to Apprehension and Assent, are complementary and mutually interactive aspects of our intellect. They exhibit the perfect harmony and cohesion existing in the operation of all our potencies whether they are those of our senses, external or internal, or of our intellect.[21] Such a view of the integral unity in the functioning of our cognitive powers concurs with that of Aquinas who affirms: 'Strictly speaking it is neither senses nor intellect that knows, but man, through both.'[22] This unity can also be seen as Newman's answer to the dangers inherent both in rationalism and empiricism. It offsets the tendency to reduce our ability to know only to that which is strictly demonstrable from a logical point of view. On the other hand, it counters the pitfall of an empiricism that would reduce our knowledge to only that which is detectable by the senses.

I think it is possible to draw a certain parallel between Newman's distinctions of Real and Notional as applied to Apprehension and Assent and similar concepts in the thought of Aquinas. The latter speaks of the ability that the intellect has of knowing individual being as such (*ratio particularis*), and of intellectual abstraction, whereby essences are separated from the individual being or beings to which they belong, giving rise to our universal concepts (*ratio universalis*).[23]

Further evidence of such a likeness is found in the way they both envisage our knowledge of concrete, individual, reality. As we have seen, Newman recognizes not only the importance of Real Apprehension in terms of our knowledge of concrete reality, but also that it is possible in many cases, through a deeper metaphysical contemplation of reality, to convert our Notional into Real Apprehension. It will be remembered that this is the context of his concept of realization in which such a transition from Notional Assent to Real Assent takes place.

A similar view is found in the thought of Aquinas. The intellect maintains, or perfects its knowledge of the individual being in reality, by constantly returning to consider the original sense information in the memory and imagination (*conversio ad phantasmata*).[24] This continual referring back (*reditio*) by the intellect to the reality from which our knowledge is derived serves as a safeguard against the possible aberrations of our imagination.[25] It also provides us with a constant reminder that our abstractions have no independent existence of their own. In this way it helps us to avoid the danger of confusing our ideas with individual reality. Without this continual reference to reality itself, constantly checking and cross-checking our concepts of it, we run the risk of inventing a virtual model rather than discovering reality in all its richness and beauty of being.

Such parallels of thought seem to be confirmed when both Aquinas and Newman subsequently reach the same conclusion. As we have seen, Newman affirms that it is the Real Assent of an individual that tends to be a stimulus for future action. Similarly, Aquinas, after discussing how 'reason directs human acts in accordance with a twofold knowledge, universal and particular',[26] concludes that: 'Universal knowledge, which is most certain, does not hold the foremost place in action, but rather particular knowledge, since actions are about singulars.'[27]

I believe that the above evidence, together with that which is found throughout his writings, shows Newman's profound appreciation for the unity of the human being. We know and act with a unity of being. There is no dichotomy between body and soul. I consider this to be one more fundamental point of coincidence with the philosophy of Aquinas.[28] It could be argued that there is nothing very original in his re-affirmation of the unity of man in all his actions. After all Aristotle and Aquinas had already given it due emphasis in their anthropologies. However, I think it can be considered to be one of

Newman's major contributions to contemporary philosophy coming as it does at a time when many thinkers are still grappling with the legacy of Descartes, and the various forms of dualism and idealism which it has spawned. It can also be seen as a positive addition to the present development of certain person-centred philosophies. That is to say, those philosophical currents which seek to highlight the nature of the human spirit as a reaction to the consequences of the rampant materialism of the age, both theoretical and practical. Such an approach to philosophy endeavours to proclaim the dignity and rights of the person. At the same time it challenges the individualism that attempts to suffocate the social nature of the human being together with his responsibilities towards the rest of the human race.

I share this conclusion with Sillem who, in the final three sentences of his masterly study of Newman's thought, writes: 'As far as philosophy is concerned he was no Augustine, Aquinas nor Scotus in stature. ... But he stands at the threshold of the new age as a Christian Socrates, the pioneer of a new philosophy of the individual Person and Personal Life.'[29]

Informal Inference

I believe that his view of Informal Inference represents another significant contribution to the development of philosophy. Newman reminds the world that we humans can know with certitude the individual and particular of reality. Such an affirmation comes as a ray of light within the cloud of scepticism still to be found in many philosophical schools. The cloud that was the result of the various tendencies towards idealism and empiricism of previous centuries.

Informal Inference enables us to know the contingent and particular of reality, 'the truth of things'.[30] In his book on the history of philosophy Copleston makes a passing reference to Newman when discussing the logic of Aristotle. He mentions that Aristotle did not consider Informal Inference, as proposed by Newman, in terms of enabling us to know the concrete and individual in reality. On the other hand, he says that 'Aquinas recognised this type of reasoning, and attributed it to the *vis cogitativa*, also called *ratio particularis*.'[31] I have also drawn attention to the presence of these specific parallels in the thought of Newman and Aquinas.

As we have seen, Informal Inference involves both deductive and inductive forms of Inference. I think that Newman's recognition of induction, as a valid form of reasoning enabling us to reach knowledge of concrete reality, shows his implicit appreciation of causality as founded on the universal participation of being. The mode of operation of Informal Inference suggests that the intellect perceives the causal relationships inherent in the formulation of the various 'independent probabilities'. Therefore, it is able to identify those that can be viewed as converging towards one particular conclusion. As Juan José Sanguineti observes, our intellectual potencies are able to detect the universal participation of being within reality. Consequently, they are able to perceive the likely presence of causal relationships within contingent reality as observed through our sense experience.[32] This enables the mind, as Newman says, to 'grasp the full tale of premises and the conclusion, *per modum unius*, – by a sort of instinctive perception of the legitimate conclusion in and through the premises'.[33]

The intellect has the ability (*ratio particularis*) to relate the conclusions of Informal Inference to concrete reality. The whole process can take place in the mind in a spontaneous way, although it is always open to the most rigorous investigation by the intellect itself. Informal Inference can produce the impression that it both begins with concrete facts and its conclusions relate to individual reality. It is only with reflection and an analysis of the mental process that it can be appreciated to have involved self-evident truths or first principles, and that it was discursive.

Informal Inference concentrates all the potencies of our intellect into knowing reality, both of individual beings (*ratio particularis*) and of the essences of beings (*ratio universalis*). However, when it comes to communicating its results to others, then by its very nature it does not have the same advantages as Formal Inference.

The Illative Sense

Norris claims that Newman's Illative Sense is 'his most original achievement'.[34] I think that in general terms, as mentioned in the previous chapter, the Illative Sense can be identified in the thought of Aquinas with the active habit of science, understood as a quality of the intellect. That the Illative Sense is not an entirely original discovery on the part of Newman does not detract from considering it as one of his major contributions to contemporary philosophy. His achievement lies in his masterly phenomenological description of its nature and in highlighting its vital role in the theory of knowledge.

As a consequence of the vast amount of research that is taking place in the world today our knowledge of the natural sciences is continually increasing. One logical result of this amazing progress is that they are continually becoming more and more specialized, with new branches of science appearing continuously. At the same time there is a constant demand for both scientific rigour in terms of verification, and for the accurate communication of the results. This usually implies the elaboration of Formal Inferences in order to provide the appropriate logical demonstrations and scientific explanations of these advances in scientific knowledge.

Newman's Illative Sense serves the useful purpose of reminding the scientific world of today that, when it comes to the verification of new discoveries, there are other factors apart from Formal Inferences that need to be borne in mind. For instance, we should question whether the scientists involved can also substantiate their claim to having a well developed Illative Sense within their particular field of research. If scientists were more aware of the role and operation of the Illative Sense then, together with expressing their findings in terms of Formal Inferences, they would also take particular care to describe the Informal Inferences that led them to their conclusions. Simultaneously, they would inform us not to expect the same rigour as demanded by Formal Inference since, by their very nature, such Informal Inferences cannot be adequately expressed. This approach would not only be helpful in supporting their Formal Inferences, but also in providing an aid in leading us in the right direction towards understanding the fruits of their investigations. Furthermore, such explanations as they were able to give would provide evidence to show that they did possess a mature Illative Sense in that particular sphere of knowledge.

The importance of taking into account the Illative Sense does not only apply to the empirical sciences. For instance, it is also necessary in the positive sciences such as historical research, and of course with respect to the advance of philosophy.

Together with Informal Inference I think that the Illative Sense bears witness to Newman's implicit awareness of the universal participation of being as constituting the foundation of causality. The Illative Sense is the active habit of the intellect which enables us to discern and appraise all the causal relationships existing in the context of our particular field of study. Since it can draw on all our existing knowledge it enables us to have an overall view (*per modum unius*) of all the causal links, however tenuous, found within the evidence, facts and inferences of whatever kind, which accumulatively converge and point towards a particular conclusion for our possible Assent. In other words, the Illative Sense makes it possible to compare and evaluate all the causal relationships, to view them as coherent with one another, to see the reasonableness of all these individual independent probabilities converging to one conclusion. And finally, on the basis of all that rational evidence, it sanctions, or not, the giving of our Assent.

The Phenomenological Movement

I believe that these insights on the unity of man, Informal Inference and the Illative Sense constitute Newman's main contribution to the progress of contemporary philosophy. However, is it possible to classify his approach in the context of the history of philosophy? It will be recalled that Copleston commented that one of the reasons why Newman is generally overlooked as a philosopher is the difficulty of finding a suitable place for his thought within the various currents of nineteenth-century philosophy.

We have also seen how Newman was very much his own man, and did not wish to be associated with any particular philosophical school of the time. However, if an appropriate classification can be found, be it ever so general, then it would facilitate his recognition as a significant contemporary philosopher.

Given the difference in life span, country and language it is highly unlikely that Newman, who died in 1890, was acquainted with the thought of Edmund Husserl (1859–1938). This would appear to be confirmed by the fact that there is no mention of him in any of his writings. Similarly, there is no evidence to show that Husserl, who lived and worked in Germany, and recognized as the founder of what is now called the phenomenological movement, had any knowledge of the philosophy of Newman. Consequently, no case can be made for thinking that Newman played any direct part whatsoever in the development of this movement. Likewise, there can be no suggestion that he was a precursor of it in the same way that Franz Brentano and Carl Stumpfit are generally recognized to have been. This is quite clear since, in the years leading up to the birth of the phenomenological movement, Newman's thinking was not generally known among professional philosophers within the German-speaking milieu.

I agree with Herbert Spiegelberg that the term phenomenology, which had gained general recognition by 1913, should not be considered as referring to a particular school of philosophy.[35] Spiegelberg explains that it is more appropriate to consider it as designating a movement since its most fundamental characteristic is its method.[36] Many of the philosophers who have embraced this methodology over the years have reached quite diverse conclusions. And on occasions even directly contradictory with one another. We only have to think, for instance, of the widely differing results arrived at by Husserl, Martin Heidegger, Max Scheler, Edith Stein, Jean-Paul Sartre and Maurice Merleau-Ponty. This in itself is sufficient to show that it is not possible to refer to phenomenology as a philosophical school. A school should at least imply a general agreement among its adherents regarding its basic concepts.

I am sure the reader, after this introduction, has guessed that I am about to propose the hypothesis that Newman's approach to philosophy shares some similarities with the phenomenological movement. I am not alone in holding such a theory. Attention has also been drawn to it by scholars such as Sillem, Walgrave, Boekraad, Artz, Norris, David Pailin and Ker.[37]

To demonstrate this theory I begin by showing the existence of some general parallels with the phenomenological movement. Newman's thought can be considered as a reaction against the then current tendencies towards empiricism and idealism. The early proponents of phenomenology were also reacting against similar tendencies. There is even a certain likeness in the careers of Newman and Husserl. At one stage Husserl took an interest in the kind of empiricism represented by Locke and Mill, as occurred with Newman. It is even more striking that, like Newman, in the course of time this evolved into a positive aversion for these ways of thinking.

Newman's realism, as we have seen, gives great importance to the knowledge of individual concrete reality: 'I would confine myself to the truth of things, and to the mind's certitude of that truth.'[38] This approach finds a distinct echo in the thought of those who took part in the beginnings of the phenomenological movement with its leitmotif of '*zu den Sachen* (to the things themselves)'. This was their response to what they considered as fossilized philosophical systems, or those constructed on the basis of idealistic prejudices. Walgrave remarks that: 'If it is true that Husserl's programme of "going back to the things themselves" is the very mark of a great philosopher, then Newman is to be considered as an outstanding genius in the history of human thought.'[39]

Commenting on the realism found in the *Grammar*, the same author says:

Just as the grammarian confines his efforts to extracting from

actual use the laws of language, so Newman aims at tracing
out the structures of thought from his observations of mental
life in its entirety, without any attempt at evaluation. ... In
other words Newman might have called his Essay *The
Phenomenology of Assent*.[40]

Another general resemblance between the methodology of
Newman and that of the phenomenological movement is his
insistence on there always being a complete openness and readi-
ness to learn from reality. To approach reality with a spirit of
wonder and discovery facilitates the elaboration of a coherent,
yet homogeneously developing philosophy. At the same time,
such an attitude is conducive to an awareness of rejecting any
temptation to tame reality by trying to enclose it within an arti-
ficially constructed logical system. Spiegelberg confirms that
this same approach is a characteristic of the phenomenological
movement:

> What distinguishes phenomenology from other methods is
> not so much any particular step it develops or adds to them
> but the spirit of philosophical reverence as the first and fore-
> most norm of the philosophical enterprise. The violation of
> this norm in an age of reductionism constituted the *raison
> d'être* for phenomenology at the time of its birth.[41]

While acknowledging these general similarities it is equally
important to highlight the differences between Newman's
thought and that of the later protagonists of the phenomenological movement. The first adherents to the movement,
represented by the Göttingen and Munich circles, soon began to
branch out along very different philosophical pathways. The
itinerary of Husserl's thought epitomizes this process. He began
with a resolute determination to seek only reality, and harshly
criticized various forms of idealism. Unfortunately, he subsequently turned to Descartes for inspiration. The final
consequence was that, as Spiegelberg explains, he himself fell
into a kind of reductionism, and his transcendental phenomenology became a phenomenological idealism.[42] Conversely,

Newman's thought developed in a generally consistent and homogeneous way. He remained ever true to his realist position that found its definitive and mature expression in the *Grammar*. Any comparison of his way of thinking with phenomenology, as Sillem also points out, must carefully exclude any form of idealism, transcendental or otherwise.[43]

Spiegelberg explains how it is perfectly feasible to employ the phenomenological method without necessarily espousing the conclusions of Husserl, Heidegger, Scheler, Sartre, or indeed any of the recognized phenomenologists.[44] There are contemporary philosophers who, while appreciating the value of the phenomenological method, have remained very definitely in the realist camp. Among such we can name Stein, Dietrich von Hildebrand and Karol Wojtyla.[45]

Descriptive Phenomenology

Thus there are some comparisons that support my theory. However, is it possible to identify more specific points of similarity with Newman's thought and the phenomenological movement? I think that there are also some clear parallels with respect to methodology and in particular with what is referred to as descriptive phenomenology within the movement.

For the sake of clarity, following the suggestion of Spiegelberg, I use the terminology descriptive phenomenology in its widest connotation as accepted by the movement itself.[46] That is to say, the method of descriptive phenomenology may be attributed to those philosophers who, being aware of the basic tenets of the phenomenological movement, would recognize them as present, in some form or other, in their own thinking. At the same time, however, they may not necessarily wish to be identified with the movement as such.

Spiegelberg distinguishes three stages in the phenomenological method that are accepted, at least implicitly, and implemented by those who have aligned themselves with the phenomenological movement.[47] He designates these three stages as: 'investigating particular phenomena'; 'investigating general essences'; and 'apprehending essential relationships among essences'. He subdivides the first of these stages into three different steps, namely, 'the intuitive grasp of the phenomena, their analytic examination, and their description'. When the first stage, regarding the investigation of some aspect of reality, has been completed then the resulting explanation is referred to as a 'phenomenological description'.

Newman does not discuss his methodology regarding philosophy in his writings. Our knowledge of his method must be derived from the analysis of his thought and his manner of expressing it. The *Grammar*, containing the most systematic and definitive account of his philosophy, provides the best illustration of his method. As we have just seen, the first stage of the phenomenological method, 'investigating particular phenomena', has as its first step 'the intuitive grasp of the phenomena'. Newman's acute observations of all the phenomena associated with our cognitive acts appear to be in full accord with this first step of 'phenomenological description'. This aspect of his realist approach is supported by his constant warnings against introducing any preconceived theories. He alerts us to the danger of indulging our imagination in our investigation of how the intellect operates, rather than a careful examination of the facts. He insists that we must consider the operations of the intellect '*in facto esse*, in contrast with *in fieri*'.[48]

His descriptions of the various elements involved in the different operations of the intellect can be seen as following the second step of the first stage: 'analytic examination'. The distinctions and divisions of the various aspects of these operations certainly constitute a thorough analysis of the cognitive process. He describes the harmony and complementary interaction of Real and Notional Apprehension; Real and Notional Assent; simple and complex Assent; Formal, Informal and Natural Inference; and the Illative Sense. His analysis of how the intellect reaches the truth of reality is not the result of trying to make the facts fit a theory, but of his endeavour to describe the actual process, '*in facto esse*', through which the intellect attains knowledge.

The third step of the first stage consists in the description of the phenomena. It is integrally related to the previous intuitive and analytic steps.[49] This description presents the conclusions derived from the first two steps, combining and clarifying all the relationships between the various elements. It should serve to guide the reader towards an experience of the phenomena, to facilitate the apprehension and understanding of the same truths. The *Grammar* seems to follow such a pattern. Its full title, *An Essay in Aid of a Grammar of Assent*, even appears to announce such a project. Newman constantly strives to lead the reader to a greater understanding of the various elements involved in the operations of the intellect. To do this effectively he makes use of appropriate illustrations. These are carefully selected to help the sympathetic reader in his appreciation of the truths being considered. He does not adopt the attitude of trying to convince by force of logic. It is clear to me that he is well aware of his use of this method in the *Grammar*. I suggest an instance where, in giving advice to the reader, he indirectly reveals his own method. After quoting some 'grand words of Aristotle', on the importance of allowing ourselves to be guided by the experience of others in a particular field of knowledge, he comments:

> We must take up their particular subject as they took it up, beginning at the beginning, give ourselves to it, depend on practice and experience more than on reasoning, and thus gain that mental insight into truth, whatever its subject-matter may be, which our masters have gained before us. By following this course, we may make ourselves of their number, and then we rightly lean upon ourselves, directing ourselves by our own moral or intellectual judgment, not by our skill in argumentation.[50]

Newman's approach is to guide the reader through Informal Inferences and Real Assents towards a greater realization of the truths of individual reality. Where, as we have seen, realization implies the deepening of our understanding of the truths of reality in all their ontological richness. I am of the opinion, together with Sillem, Boekraad and Norris, that the importance he gives to realization forms an integral part of his phenomeno-logical approach.[51]

From this evidence it is clear that there do exist affinities between Newman's methodology and that of 'phenomeno-logical description'. Further evidence is forthcoming if we examine in more detail his approach to any particular aspect of reality. The Illative Sense plays a central role in his theory of knowledge. I have also argued that his phenomenological description of it constitutes one of his major contributions to contemporary philosophy. Therefore, this aspect of the opera-tion of the intellect can provide us with an appropriate case to examine, whether or not, his method of presenting it follows the pattern identifiable with 'phenomenological description'.

He divides his chapter on the Illative Sense in the *Grammar* into three sections: '1. The Sanction of the Illative Sense'; '2. The Nature of the Illative Sense'; '3. The Range of the Illative Sense'. It would be presumptuous to claim that these three sections correspond exactly to the three steps of the first stage of the phenomenological method. However, a close examination of them certainly reveals some interesting parallels.

For instance, the first section on 'The Sanction of the Illative Sense' deals with the existence, and evidence of such a phenom-enon, following an intuitive approach. On contemplating our human nature Newman finds that, like the other living beings found in the world, it must include within it all that is necessary for it to flourish within the reality of which it is part. And, in the case of the human being, the acquisition of truth is necessary for achieving perfection, 'his progress is a living growth, not a mechanism; and its instruments are mental acts, not the formu-las and contrivances of language'.[52]

Accordingly, the existence of a function of the human intel-lect, designated as the Illative Sense, is based on the consid-eration of our rational nature as it operates in practice. The manner in which he introduces the Illative Sense certainly seems to be in accord with the first step of the phenomeno-logical method, namely, 'the intuitive grasp of the pheno-mena'.

In a similar way his second section, 'The Nature of the Illa-

tive Sense', can be seen as an 'analytic examination'. The Illative Sense is the ability of the intellect to know when it is truly
reasonable to give, to a conditional conclusion in some field of
knowledge, an unconditional Assent. He compares and contrasts
the Illative Sense with what he refers to as 'parallel faculties'.
As we have seen, he takes his first example from the thought of
Aristotle. He compares the Illative Sense with *phronesis* which
Aristotle describes as the acquired habit that enables us judge
with respect to all those matters related to the achievement of
our own personal good. Newman explains that the Illative Sense
operates in an analogous way, but with respect to the truth. He
describes how, just as *phronesis* manifests varying degrees of
development within the different spheres of human activity, so
the Illative Sense may be more developed in one domain of
knowledge than another. He continues his analysis by examining further similarities with other 'parallel faculties'.

At the end of this second section he gives a summary of the
results of his analytical examination regarding the nature of the
Illative Sense. It seems to me that this summary, divided into
four parts, can be considered as the beginning of the third step,
the descriptive step, of his phenomenological description of the
Illative Sense. He commences by saying that it is present in all
the operations of our intellect and with respect to all fields of
knowledge. He then remarks that in practice, according to our
experience and personal effort, it becomes more developed as a
habit of the intellect in some areas rather than others. Thirdly,
that it operates using Informal Inference where the conclusion is
given in the limit of an 'accumulation of probabilities'. The final
characteristic of the Illative Sense which he describes is that of
its function to give or withhold Assent to such a conclusion as
true.

In the last section, 'The Range of the Illative Sense', Newman
elaborates on his phenomenological description. He explains its
role in more detail with respect to the different operations of the
intellect. He describes its function with respect to our fundamental attitude or intellectual approach to reality, with the
attainment of self-evident truths and first principles on which
our Inferences rely. He then discusses the part it plays with

respect to the different kinds of Inferences themselves, and finally with how it sanctions our Assent to a particular conclusion. Throughout his explanation he provides examples to illustrate the role of the Illative Sense. It is clear that he is trying to lead the reader towards a deeper realization of its nature. We can say that with this last section he completes his 'description', the third step required for the method of 'phenomenological description'.

This appraisal of his way of describing the Illative Sense reveals that he does follow the three steps which constitute the first stage of 'investigating particular phenomena'. He begins by describing the phenomenon itself from an intuitive point of view. He proceeds with an analytic examination of its nature. And finally, he gives a descriptive summary of his conclusions, complete with illustrations to help the reader in his realization of the nature of the Illative Sense. Thus, I think we are justified in saying that he has produced a 'phenomenological description' of the Illative Sense.

According to Spiegelberg the second stage of the phenomenological method entails 'investigating general essences' or 'eidetic intuiting'.[53] In the terminology familiar to students of Aquinas this stage suggests the consideration of universal concepts as a result of intellectual abstraction with respect to the reality under investigation. In his *Grammar* Newman continually reminds us of the difference between Real and Notional with respect to both Apprehension and Assent. Also, he is constantly drawing our attention to the difference between the individual beings of reality and our intellectual abstractions of their essences. At least this appears to imply that he would be sympathetic to this second stage of the phenomenological method. Further evidence for this is shown by his appreciation of the important role of universal concepts in our Formal Inferences essential for the progress of science. However, since his specific interest in the *Grammar* is to establish how we can have certitude with respect to concrete reality, we cannot say that he followed this aspect of the methodology simply because it was not included within his overall philosophical aim.

Spiegelberg refers to the third stage of the phenomenological method as 'apprehending essential relationships among essences'.[54] For the same reason just given regarding the second stage it is not possible to credit Newman as complying with the criteria of this third stage. Nevertheless, his analysis of the internal relationships between the various forms of Notional Assent could be regarded as an instance of this stage. I refer to his classification of the various kinds of Notional Assent into Profession, Credence, Opinion, Presumption and Speculation. As we have seen, this division is based on specific differences with respect to the Apprehension of the given reality as expressed in the proposition of the Notional Assent. Another such example could be his division of Notional Assent into 'simple' and 'complex' with their corresponding descriptions.

Among other characteristics of the phenomenological method Spiegelberg speaks of 'suspending belief in the existence of the phenomena'.[55] Such a phenomenological reductionism became a characteristic of Husserl's methodology. However, it has not been universally accepted by those associated with the phenomenological movement. Newman's realism, as we have seen, does not admit any methodical doubt.

It is not relevant to compare Newman's method with any additional aspects of the phenomenological movement. Spiegelberg affirms that, as such, these are not considered as forming part of the basic tenets of the movement. He states that only the first three stages are generally 'accepted, at least implicitly, and practised by all those who have aligned themselves with the phenomenological movement; the later ones only by a smaller group'.[56]

From this evidence we can conclude that there are some very definite parallels between Newman's methodology and that of the phenomenological movement. Firstly, there are those in terms of the general approach to philosophy. Secondly, we have found clear similarities with respect to methodology. These are such that it is possible to identify specific elements in that of Newman which satisfy the criteria of the phenomenological movement. Thus we are justified in referring to his method as 'phenomenological description'. And finally, on examining the particular case of the Illative Sense, we have seen that it fulfils these same criteria for his method to be called descriptive phenomenology. In other words, there is sufficient evidence to demonstrate my hypothesis that Newman's approach does include elements in common with the phenomenological movement. Furthermore, that his methodology satisfies the criteria of this movement such that it can be designated as descriptive phenomenology.

Sillem goes so far as to say that the evidence warrants the claim that Newman was 'at least a forerunner of the Phenomenologists of the present day'.[57] I think that at least we can speculate that if he had been a professional philosopher, working and teaching at the University of Oxford, then it would have only been a question of time before being recognized as having provided some of the groundwork for the phenomenological movement. Alternatively, if he had lived and worked in Germany, or even if his *Grammar* had been immediately translated into German, then the probability of his recognition as a forerunner of the phenomenological movement, like Brentano and Stumpf, would have been even higher.

Although I would not go as far as Sillem I do think that the evidence shows that Newman was a latent forerunner of the phenomenological movement. The acceptance of this conclusion would mean that the quest for a philosophical label for him in terms of contemporary trends has been accomplished. We are able to designate Newman as a latent forerunner of the phenomenological movement. And that his philosophical method can be given the general classification of descriptive phenomenology as it is understood today. Such a classification provides him with a definite place in the history of contemporary philosophy. Furthermore, to be known as a latent forerunner of the phenomenological movement would serve to enhance his recognition as a notable philosopher of the nineteenth century.

Apart from providing us with a useful label we might ask whether his latent association with the phenomenological movement brings with it any other benefit. Spiegelberg, in his consideration of 'the outlook for the future of the *phenomeno-*

logical movement', admits that it may not be able to answer the ultimate metaphysical questions. However, he adds that 'for such an assignment its resources may be necessary'.[58] A phenomenology that remains ever open to reality can prove itself a useful instrument in the elaboration of a realist metaphysics. Sillem is of the same opinion, and concludes:

> Thus Newman's phenomenological method is the way of approach he created for a metaphysics of being. His descriptive analyses of personal experience serve the Thomist metaphysician well for they flow naturally into St Thomas's science of all things considered as beings, and situate the whole fabric of his system in the world of things and persons.[59]

While being careful not to exaggerate I also feel that his phenomenological approach to reality can be of service to the realist metaphysician.

Champion of Realism

Copleston, in the final paragraph of his survey of Newman's philosophy, describes his importance in the following terms: 'The growth of interest in his philosophical thought ... has coincided with the spread of movements in philosophy ... which, on our looking back, are seen to have certain affinities with elements in Newman's reflections.'[60] Are there any other currents in philosophy, apart from the phenomenological movement, that may be related to his thought?

I think it is reasonable to consider his philosophy as part of the response against the extreme empiricism and idealism which occurred towards the end of the nineteenth century. This reaction proved to be the catalyst in the formation of a trend towards realism which took place specfically in Britain and the United States. This movement later became known as Oxford philosophy and is associated in particular with the thought of Bertrand Russell (1872–1970), George Edward Moore (1873–1958) and

Ludwig Wittgenstein (1889–1951).

There does not appear to be any direct relationship between the thought of Newman and this trend towards realism. However, his approach does represent a direct attack against the empiricism and idealism currently in vogue at the time. He is fully aware that empiricism leads to a reductionism regarding human knowledge and strove to dispel the legacy of empiricism left by Hobbes, Locke, Berkeley and Hume. On the other hand, his realist approach to knowledge shines out amidst the idealisms proposed by Kant, Hegel, Fichte, Schelling and their followers.

It may be possible to find some specific evidence to show that Newman could be included among the Oxford pioneers of this realist movement. It is not unreasonable to suppose that the *Grammar*, published in 1870, could have come to the attention of any of these Oxford men thus providing inspiration for their own thought. If this could be demonstrated then Newman would merit a place among the ranks of the forerunners of Oxford philosophy, men such as Thomas Case (1844–1925), John Cook Wilson (1849–1915), Alfred North Whitehead (1861–1947), Horace William Brindley Joseph (1867–1943) and Harold Arthur Prichard (1871–1947).

What is beyond doubt is that Newman kept a light burning for the cause of realism among the shadows of nineteenth-century philosophy. Sillem rightly adds that his stand for realism is all the more significant since he was almost alone at the time.[61]

Significance Today

I pointed out in my first chapter that over the past few decades the philosophy of Newman has gradually attracted more and more serious attention. In this context I mentioned authors such as Jean Guitton, Etienne Gilson, A. J. Boekraad, Bernard Lonergan, Jan Hendrik Walgrave, James Collins, Frederick Copleston, Edward Sillem, Johannes Artz, Ian Ker and Stanley L. Jaki. This growing interest shows that his thought is becoming more generally recognized as relevant to philosophy today.

In this final chapter I have presented what I consider to be his major contributions to the development of philosophy. These include his profound appreciation for the unity of the human being in all his actions together with his view on Informal Inference and the Illative Sense. I have shown that he can be given a philosophical label, that of a latent forerunner of the phenomenological movement. Finally, I have suggested the feasibility of him being included among the pioneers of the realist movement that became known as Oxford philosophy. Thus, together with Newman's positive additions to the progress of philosophy, we have at least one clear classification for his thought that would facilitate his insertion in the history books.

The overall intention of this book is to show that John Henry Newman, apart from his deserved fame as a theologian, also merits universal recognition as a significant contemporary philosopher. And therefore should be included in the ranks of the more distinguished philosophers of the nineteenth century.

Having read the evidence presented in these pages it is up to the reader to give his own verdict. In my appraisal of his philosophy and approach to knowledge I have endeavoured to present this evidence as objectively as possible.

I think that the influence that Newman's thought may have on the future of philosophy can best be expressed in some of his own words. Commenting on the genius of Francis Bacon he says, 'whose speculations about physical fact and law are of all sorts, thrown out with great profusion and variety, as seeds scattered over the field of inquiry, and left for the event to determine which will prosper and which will not'.[62] I feel that these sentiments, referring to the wonders of science in which Bacon was a pioneer, could equally be applied to Newman's philosophical reflections. Time will tell what fruitful consequences will come from his prodigious sowing in the field of philosophy.

Notes

1. Copleston, vol. VIII, p. 525.

2. Sillem, p. 31 footnote 3, in *Phil N* II.
3. Cf. Gilson, *Elements of Christian Philosophy*, pp. 260–2.
4. Cf. a selection from many possible examples: *US*, pp. 256–7, 344; *Apo*, pp. 30, 169; *GA*, pp. 59–60 (83), 196 (303), 201 (310), 205 (316), 214 (331), 223 (345), 226 (350), 227–8 (353), 232 (360), 248 (384), 263–4 (409–10); *TP* I, pp. 48, 88, 126; *Phil N* II, pp. 29, 87.
5. *GA*, p. 224 (346).
6. Cf. Sillem, pp. 8, 14–15, 73–96, 133–4; Norris, pp. 14–16, 41–2.
7. *TP* I, p. 39.
8. *Apo*, p. 169; cf. ibid., pp. 103, 168.
9. *GA*, p. 227 (353); cf. ibid., pp. 136, 230, 240.
10. *GA*, p. 67 (94); cf. ibid., pp. 224–5 (348); *US*, 253.
11. *GA*, p. 224 (346); cf. *PS* IV, pp. 201–2; *US*, p. 198; *Phil N* II, pp. 25, 93–9.
12. *GA*, p. 206 (318).
13. *TP* I, p. 155; cf. ibid., p. 154.
14. Cf. Sillem, pp. 93–4.
15. Jaki, *The Purpose of It All*, pp. 224–5.
16. *GA*, p.112 (169); cf. ibid., pp. 196–7 (302–3), 207 (320), 258 (400), 266 (413); *Dev*, pp. 44–5; *TP* I, pp. 15, 126; *Phil N* II, p. 169; *Prepos.* pp. 277–91; *Apo*, p. 230.
17. *GA*, p. 202 (311).
18. *GA*, p. 274 (426).
19. Letter to Coleridge, quoted in Ward, vol. II, p. 270.
20. Cf. Aquinas, *Summa Theologiae* I, q. 1, a. 6 ad 3; ibid., *Summa Contra Gentiles* I, c. 95; ibid., *De Veritate*, q. 24, a. 8; ibid., *De Malo,* q. 3, a. 7; ibid., *In II Sent.*, d. 39, q. 1, a. 2, *corpus* and a. 2 ad 3; ibid., *In II Sent.*, d. 43, q. 1, a. 1 ad 3.
21. Cf. *GA*, pp. 29–30 (34–5), 47–8 (62–4), *passim*; *TP* I, p. 39.
22. Aquinas, *De Veritate*, q. 2, a. 6 ad 3: 'Non enim, proprie loquendo, sensus ut intellectus cognoscit, sed homo per utrum-que'; cf. ibid., q. 2, a. 6, *corpus*.
23. Cf. Aquinas, *Summa Theologiae* I, q. 14, a. 11; q. 78, a. 4; q. 85, a. 3; q. 86, a. 1; ibid., *Summa Theologiae* I–II, q. 76, a. 1; q. 77, a. 2 ad 1; ibid., *Summa Theologiae* I–II, q. 2, a. 1.
24. Cf. Aquinas, *Summa Theologiae* I. q. 84, a. 7; ibid., *De Veritate*, q. 2, a. 6 ad 3.
25. Cf. Aquinas, *De Veritate*, q. 1, a. 9.
26. Aquinas, *Summa Theologiae* I–II, q. 76, a. 1, *corpus*.
27. Aquinas, *Summa Theologiae* I–II, q. 77, a. 2 ad 1.

28. Cf. Aquinas, *Summa Theologiae* I, q. 75, a. 7 ad 3; q. 76, a. 1, *corpus*; and a. 1 ad 4–5, also a. 8, *corpus*; ibid., *De Veritate*, q. 15, a. 1, *corpus*; ibid., *Summa Contra Gentiles* II, c. 68; ibid., *De Spiritualibus Creaturis*, a. 2 ad 3.

29. Sillem, p. 250; cf. ibid., pp. 133–4.

30. *GA*, p. 223 (344); cf. *TP* I, p. 19.

31. Copleston, vol. I, p. 284.

32. Cf. Sanguineti, pp. 183, 286–7.

33. *GA*, p. 196 (301–2).

34. Norris, p. 42.

35. Cf. Spiegelberg, pp. xxvii–xxviii, 1–2, 5.

36. Cf. Spiegelberg, pp. 5–7, 22, 653–6.

37. Cf. Sillem, pp. 19, 75, 127–39; Walgrave, *Newman. Le développement du dogme*, p. 82; Boekraad, *The Personal Conquest of Truth*, pp. 137–40; Artz, 'Newman as Philosopher', pp. 282–3; Artz, 'Preface', in Norris, p. xiii; Norris, pp. 14–16, 27–8; Pailin, pp. 186–7; Ker, 'Introduction', in *GA* (1985), p. lv.

38. *GA*, p. 223 (344).

39. Walgrave, *Unfolding Revelation*, p. 297.

40. Walgrave, *Newman. Le développement du dogme*, p. 82.

41. Spiegelberg, p. 701; cf. ibid., pp. 75–88, 635–6.

42. Cf. Spiegelberg, pp. 91–163, 649.

43. Cf. Sillem, pp. 75, 127–39.

44. Cf. Spiegelberg, p. 404.

45. Cf. Spiegelberg, pp. 222–4; Buttiglione, pp. 305–14; Wojtyla, *The Acting Person*.

46. Cf. Spiegelberg, p. 6.

47. Cf. Spiegelberg, pp. 658–9.

48. *GA*, p. 222 (343).

49. Cf. Spiegelberg, pp. 672–6.

50. *GA*, p. 221 (342).

51. Cf. Sillem, p. 136; Boekraad, *The Personal Conquest of Truth*, pp. 138–40; Norris, p. 16.

52. *GA*, p. 226 (350); cf. ibid., pp. 227–8 (353).

53. Cf. Spiegelberg, pp. 676–9.

54. Cf. Spiegelberg, pp. 680–4.

55. Cf. Spiegelberg, pp. 690–4.

56. Spiegelberg, p. 659.

57. Sillem, p. 135.

58. Spiegelberg, p. 643.

59. Sillem, p. 139; cf. ibid., pp. 77, 129.

60. Copleston, vol. VIII, p. 525.
61. Cf. Sillem, pp. 75, 78, 84.
62. *TP* I, p. 118.

BIBLIOGRAPHY

Works of Newman

The following list includes those referred to in this book. They are arranged in alphabetical order according to the abbreviations. The date of first publication appears in brackets. Fuller bibliographical details, including manuscript sources, can be found in the following: Charles Stephen Dessain (ed.), *The Letters and Diaries of John Henry Newman*; John Coulson, *Newman and the Common Tradition: A Study in the Language of Church and Society* (Oxford, 1970); Dwight Culler, *The Imperial Intellect: A Study of Newman's Educational Ideal* (New Haven, 1955); Vincent Ferrer Blehl, *John Henry Newman: A Bibliographical Catalogue of His Writings* (Virginia, 1978); Heinrich Fries, Werner Becker and Günter Biemer (eds), *Newman-Studien* (Glock und Lutz, Nürnberg, Germany, first vol. 1948). Further information can also be found at www.newmanfriendsinternational.org and www.newmanreader.org.

Apo: *Apologia pro Vita Sua* (1864).

AW: *John Henry Newman: Autobiographical Writings*, introduction by Henry Tristam (ed.) (Sheed and Ward, London, New York, 1956).

Dev: *An Essay on the Development of Christian Doctrine* (1845).

Diff I, II: *Certain Difficulties Felt by Anglicans in Catholic Teaching* (1850, 1875), 2 vols.

Ess I, II: *Essays Critical and Historical* (1871), 2 vols.

GA: *An Essay in Aid of a Grammar of Assent* (1870), introduction and notes, Ian Ker (ed.) (Clarendon Press, Oxford, 1985).

Gregorianum: 'The Newman-Perrone Paper on Development (*De Catholici dogmatis evolutione*)' (1847), *Gregorianum*, (T. Lynch (ed.)), Rome, 1935, vol. 16, pp. 402–47.

HS I, II, III: *Historical Sketches* (1872–1876), 3 vols.

Idea: *The Idea of a University Defined and Illustrated* (1852).

LD I–XXXI: *The Letters and Diaries of John Henry Newman*, Charles Stephen Dessain et al. (eds), vols I–VI (Clarendon Press, Oxford, 1978–1984), XI–XXII (Oxford University Press, London, 1961–1971), XXIII–XXXI (Clarendon Press, Oxford, 1973–1977), 31 vols.

Mir I, II: *Two Essays on Biblical and on Ecclesiastical Miracles* (1870), 2 vols.

Mix: *Discourses Addressed to Mixed Congregations* (1849).

Moz I, II: *Letters and Correspondence of John Henry Newman During His Life in the English Church*, Anne Mozley (ed.) (London, 1891), 2 vols.

OA: Birmingham Oratory Archives.

OS: *Sermons Preached on Various Occasions* (1857).

Phil N II: *The Philosophical Notebook of John Henry Newman*, vol. II, *The Text*, with notes by Edward Sillem and A. J. Boekraad (eds) (Nauwelaerts Publishing House, Mgr Ladeuzeplein 2, Louvain, Belgium, 1970).

Prepos: *Lectures on the Present Position of Catholics in England* (1851).

PS I–VIII: *Parochial and Plain Sermons* (1869), 8 vols.

SD: *Sermons Bearing on Subjects of the Day* (1843).

SE: *Stray Essays on Controversial Points* (1890).

TP I: *The Theological Papers of John Henry Newman on Faith and Certainty*, Hugo M. de Achaval and J. Derek Holmes (eds) (Clarendon Press, Oxford, 1976).

TP II: *Theological Papers of John Henry Newman on Biblical Inspiration and on Infallibility*, J. Derek Holmes (ed.) (Oxford, 1979).

US: *Fifteen Sermons Preached Before the University of Oxford* (1843).

OTHER AUTHORS

These include all books and articles referred to in the text, or endnotes, together with others of interest.

Aquinas, Thomas, *Summa Theologiae*, etc., Blackfriars Latin-English edn (McGraw-Hill, New York, Eyre and Spottiswoode, London, 1963), 60 vols.

Aristotle, *The Nicomachean Ethics* (The Loeb Classical Library, Harvard University Press, Cambridge, Massachusetts, 1926, revised edn 1934).

Artz, Johannes, 'Realizing', *Newman-Studien* II, 1954.

Artz, Johannes, 'Newman's Contribution to the Theory of Knowledge', *Philosophy Today*, 1960, number 4.

Artz, Johannes, 'Newman as Philosopher', *International Philosophical Quarterly*, New York, September 1976, number 16.

Artz, Johannes, 'Newman's Philosophical Achievement', *Newman-Studien* X, 1978.

Bacchus, Francis J., 'How to Read the Grammar of Assent', *The Month*, 1924, number 143.

Becker, Werner, 'Realisïerung und "Realizing" bei John Henry Newman', *Newman-Studien* V, 1962.

Benard, Edmond Darvil, *A Preface to Newman's Theology* (Herder Book Company, London, 1946).

Boekraad, A. J., *The Personal Conquest of Truth According to J. H. Newman* (Nauwelaerts, Louvain, Belgium, 1955).

Boekraad, A. J., notes to *The Philosophical Notebook of John Henry Newman*, vol. II, *The Text* (Nauwelaerts Publishing House, Mgr Ladeuzeplein 2, Louvain, Belgium, 1970).

Boekraad, A. J., 'Grammar of Assent: Observations in the Margin', *Newman-Studien* IX, 1974.

Bouyer, Louis, *Newman: His Life and Spirituality* (Meridian Books, New York, 1958).

Briodckel, A., 'Cardinal Newman's Theory of Knowledge', *American Catholic Quarterly*, 1918, number 43.

Butler, Joseph, *The Analogy of Religion, Natural and Revealed, to the Constitution and Course of Nature* (1736) (Macmillan, London, 1900).

Buttiglione, Rocco, *Il Pensiero di Karol Wojtyla* (Jaca Book, Milan, 1982).

Cameron, J. M., 'Newman and the Empiricist Tradition', in John Coulson and A. M. Allchin (eds), *The Rediscovery of Newman: An Oxford Symposium* (SPCK, London, 1967).

Cameron, J. M., 'Newman and Locke. A Note on Some Themes in an Essay in Aid of a Grammar of Assent', *Newman-Studien* IX, 1974.

Chadwick, Owen, *From Bossuet to Newman* (Cambridge University Press, Cambridge, UK, 1957).

Chalybäus, H. M., *Historical Development of Speculative Philosophy from Kant to Hegel* (T. & T. Clark, Edinburgh, 1854).

Collins, James, *Philosophical Readings in Cardinal Newman* (Henry Regnery Company, Chicago, 1961).

Copleston, Frederick, *A History of Philosophy* (Burns and Oates, London, 1966), vols I-VIII.

Coulson, John, *Newman and the Common Tradition: A Study in the Language of Church and Society* (Oxford, 1970).

Cronin, J. F., *Cardinal Newman: His Theory of Knowledge* (Catholic University of America Press, Washington, 1935).

Culler, A. Dwight, *The Imperial Intellect* (Yale University Press, New Haven, USA, 1955).

Davis, H. F., 'Newman and Thomism', *Newman-Studien* III, 1957.

D'Arcy, Martin C., *The Nature of Belief* (Sheed and Ward, London, 1937).

De Smet, W., 'L'influence de Butler sur la théorie de la foi chez Newman', *Newman-Studien* VI, 1964.

Dessain, Charles Stephen, 'Cardinal Newman on the Theory and Practice of Knowledge. The Purpose of the Grammar of Assent', *Downside Review*, January 1957, number 75.

Dessain, Charles Stephen, *John Henry Newman* (Nelson, The Birmingham Oratory, London, 1966).

Evans, G. R., 'Science and Mathematics in Newman's Thought', *Downside Review*, October 1978, number 96/325.

Evans, G. R., 'Newman and Aquinas on Assent', *Journal of Theological Studies*, April 1979, XXX/1.

Fairbairn, Andrew Martin, 'Catholicism and Modern Thought', *The Contemporary Review*, October 1885, number 47.

Ferreira, M. Jamie, *Doubt and Religious Commitment: The Role of the Will in Newman's Thought* (Clarendon Press, Oxford, 1980).

Fey, William R., *Faith and Doubt. The Unfolding of Newman's Thought on Certainty* (Patmos Press, Shepherdstown, West Virginia, USA, 1976).

Flanagan, Philip, *Newman, Faith and the Believer* (Sands, London, 1946).

Fries, Heinrich, *Die Religionsphilosophie Newmans* (1948).

Gilley, Sheridan, *Newman and His Age* (Darton, Longman and Todd, London, 1990).

Gilson, Etienne, 'Introduction', in *GA* (Image Books, Doubleday, New York, 1955).

Gilson, Etienne, *The Unity of Philosophical Experience* (Sheed and Ward, London, 1955).

Gilson, Etienne, *Being and Some Philosophers* (Europe Printing, The Hague, Holland, 1961).

Gilson, Etienne, *Elements of Christian Philosophy* (Mentor-Omega Books, Doubleday and Co., Inc., New York, 1963).

Gilson, Etienne, *Thomist Realism and the Critique of Knowledge* (Ignatius Press, San Francisco, 1986).

Guitton, Jean, *La Philosophie de Newman* (Hatier, Paris, 1933).

Harrold, Charles Frederick, 'Introduction', in *GA* (Longmans, Green and Company, New York, London, Toronto, 1947).

Haverty, Peter F., *A Thomist Interpretation and Critique of Cardinal Newman's Solution to the Problem of Assent: the Illative Sense* (Pontifical Lateran University, Rome, 1961).

Holloway, John, *The Victorian Sage* (Macmillan, London, 1953).

Jaki, Stanley L., 'Newman's Assent to Reality, Natural and Supernatural', in Stanley Jaki (ed.), *Newman Today* (Ignatius Press, San Francisco, 1989).

Jaki, Stanley L., *The Purpose of It All* (Scottish Academic Press, Edinburgh, 1990).

Jaki, Stanley L., 'Newman and Science', *The Downside Review*, 1990, number 108/373.

Jaki, Stanley L., *Newman's Challenge* (William B. Eerdmans Publishing Company, Grand Rapids, Michigan, USA, and Cambridge, UK, 2000).

Juergens, Sylvester P., 'What is Newman's Deepest Message?', *The Ecclesiastical Review*, 1928, vol. LXXVII.

Juergens, Sylvester P., *Newman on the Psychology of Faith in the Individual* (The Macmillan Company, New York, 1928).

Kenny, Anthony, 'Newman as a Philosopher of Religion', in David Brown (ed.), *Newman: a Man for Our Time* (SPCK, London, 1990).

Ker, Ian, 'Newman on Truth', *Irish Theological Quarterly*, January 1977, number 44.

Ker, Ian, 'Recent Critics of Newman's, *A Grammar of Assent'*, *Religious Studies*, March 1977, number 13.

Ker, Ian, 'Introduction', in *GA* (Oxford University Press, Clarendon Press, Oxford, 1985).

Ker, Ian, *John Henry Newman. A Biography* (Oxford University Press, Clarendon Press, Oxford, 1988 and New York, 1990).

Ker Ian, *The Achievement of John Henry Newman* (Collins, London, 1990).

Kingsley, Charles, 'What, then, does Dr. Newman Mean?', *MacMillan's Magazine,* January 1864.

Locke, John, *An Essay Concerning Human Understanding*, (London, 1690); 18th edn (London, 1788); A. C. Frazer (ed.), (Clarendon Press, Oxford, 1894), 2 vols; reprint of the 5th edn (J. W. Yolton, New York-London, 1961), 2 vols.

Lonergan, Bernard, *Insight: A Study of Human Understanding* (University of Toronto Press, Toronto, 1957, 1997).

Lonergan, Bernard, *Collection. Papers by Bernard Lonergan*, F. E. Crowe (ed.) (London, 1967).

Lonergan, Bernard, *Proceedings of the American Catholic Philosophical Society* (Washington, 1967).

Merrigan, Terrence, *Clear Heads and Holy Hearts. The Religious and Theological Ideal of John Henry Newman* (Louvain Theological and Pastoral Monographs (7), Peeters Press, Louvain, Belgium, 1991).

Mill, John Stuart, *A System of Logic, Ratiocinative and Inductive* (1843) (London, 1949).

Mitchell, Basil, 'Newman as a Philosopher', in Ian Ker and Alan G. Hill (eds), *Newman After a Hundred Years* (Clarendon Press, Oxford, 1990).

Moleski, Martin X., 'Illative Sense and Tacit Knowledge. A Comparison of the Theological Implications of the Epistemologies of John Henry Newman and Michael Polanyi', in Michael E. Allsopp, Ronald Burke (eds), *John Henry Newman. Theology and Reform* (Garland Publishing, New York, 1992).

Morales, José, 'El concepto de Teología en John Henry Newman', *Scripta Theologica*, 1969, vol. I, fasc. 2.

Morales, José, *Newman, el camino hacia la fe católica (1826–1845)* (Ediciones Universidad de Navarra, Pamplona, Spain, 1978).

Morales, José, 'John Henry Newman y el movimiento de Oxford (II)', *Scripta Theologica*, 1979, vol. XI, fasc. 3.

Morales, José, *Newman (1801–1890), forjadores de historia* (Ediciones Rialp, Madrid, 1990).

Nédoncelle, Maurice, *La Philosophie religieuse de John Henry Newman* (Société Strasbourgeoise de Librairie, Strasbourg, France, 1946).

Newton, Isaac, *Sir Isaac Newton's Mathematical Principles of Natural Philosophy and his System of the World* (English translation of Newton's *Principia Matematica* by Andrew Motte and Florian Cajori, Berkeley, California, 1947).

Newman-Studien, journal containing essays on the thought of Newman derived from the International Newman Congresses, Heinrich Fries, Werner Becker and G. Biemier (eds) (Glock und Lutz, Nürnberg, Germany, 1948–).

Norris, Thomas J., *Newman and His Theological Method. A Guide for the Theologian Today* (E. J. Brill, Leiden, Holland, 1977).

O'Connell, M. R., 'Antecedent Probability and "A Grammar of Assent"', *The New Scholasticism*, 1987, number 61/1–3.

O'Donoghue, N. D., 'Newman and the Problem of Privileged Access to Truth', *The Irish Theological Quarterly*, October 1975, number 42.

Olive, M. M., 'Comment c'est pose a Newman le probleme de l'assentiment?', *Newman-Studien* IX, 1974.

Owen, H. P., *The Christian Knowledge of God* (London, 1969).

Pailin, David A., *The Way to Faith (An Examination of Newman's "Grammar of Assent" as a Response to the Search for Certainty in Faith)* (Epworth Press, London, 1969).

Polanyi, Michael, *Personal Knowledge: Towards a Post-Critical Philosophy* (London, 1958; University of Chicago, Chicago, 1974).

Polanyi, Michael, in Michael E. Allsopp and Ronald Burke (eds), *John Henry Newman. Theology and Reform* (Garland Publishing, New York, 1992).

Price, H. H., *Belief* (G. Allan and Unwin, London, 1969).

Reid, Thomas, *Collected Works. Essays on the Intellectual Powers of Man* (Hamilton, Edinburgh, 1858).

Richardson, Laurence George, 'Newman and the Phenomenological Movement', *Acta Philosophica*, 1999, vol. 8, fasc. II.

Sanguineti, Juan José, *La filosofía de la ciencia según Santo Tomás* (Ediciones Universidad de Navarra, Pamplona, Spain, 1977).

Selby, Robin C., *The Principle of Reserve in the Writings of John Henry Cardinal Newman* (Oxford University Press, Oxford, 1975).

Sillem, Edward, *The Philosophical Notebook of John Henry Newman*, vol. I, *General Introduction to the Study of Newman's Philosophy* (Nauwelaerts Publishing House, Mgr Ladeuzeplein 2, Louvain, Belgium, 1969).

Sillem, Edward, notes in *The Philosophical Notebook of John Henry Newman*, vol. II, *The Text* (Nauwelaerts Publishing House, Mgr Ladeuzeplein 2, Louvain, Belgium, 1970).

Spiegelberg, Herbert, *The Phenomenological Movement*, 2nd edn (Martinus Nijhoff, The Hague, Holland, 1969).

Steinberg, Eric, 'Newman's Distinction Between Inference and Assent', *Religious Studies*, 1987, number 23/3.

Tracy, David, *The Achievement of Bernard Lonergan* (Herder and Herder, New York, 1970).

Trevor, Meriol, *Newman. The Pillar of the Cloud* (Macmillan Co., London, 1962).

Trevor, Meriol, *John Henry Newman, Light in Winter* (Macmillan Co., London, 1962).

Tristam, Henry, 'Introduction', in Philip Flanagan, *Newman, Faith and the Believer* (Sands, London, 1946).

Vargish, Thomas, *Newman. The Contemplation of Mind* (Oxford University Press, London, 1973).

Vince, Samuel, *The Elements of Astronomy, Designed for the Use of Students in the University*, 4th edn (Cambridge, 1816).

Walgrave, Jan Hendrik, 'L'Actualité de Newman', *Newman-Studien* III, 1957.

Walgrave, Jan Hendrik, *Newman. Le développement du dogme* (Casterman, Tournai, Paris, 1957); English translation by A. V. Littledale, *Newman the Theologian* (Sheed and Ward, New York, 1960).

Walgrave, Jan Hendrik, *Unfolding Revelation* (Westminster, London, 1972).

Walgrave, Jan Hendrik, '"Real" and "Notional" in Blondel and Newman', *Louvain Studies*, 1987, number 12.

Ward, Wilfred P., *The Life of John Henry Cardinal Newman* (Longmans Green and Company, London, 1912), 2 vols.

Whately, Richard, *The Elements of Logic* (1826; Longman, London, 1897).

Whately, Richard, *Elements of Rhetoric*, (Oxford, 1828; J. Monroe, 1861).

Wiedmann, F., 'Theorie des realen Denken nach John Henry Newman', *Newman-Studien* IV, 1960.

Willam, Franz Michel, 'Die pholosophischen Grundpositionen Newmans', *Newman-Studiun* III, 1957.

Willam, Franz Michel, *Aristotelische Erkentuislehre bei Whately und Newman* (Herder, Vienna, 1960).

Willam, Franz Michel, 'Aristotelische Bausteine der Entwicklungstheorie Newmans', *Newman-Studien* VI, 1964.

Wojtyla, Karol, O*soba I czyn* (Polskie Towarzystwo Teologiczne, Kraków, Poland, 1969); English translation, *The Acting Person* (D. Reidal Publishing Company, Dordrect, Holland, London, 1979).

Wood, James, *The Principles of Mechanics: Designed for the Use of Students in the University*, 5 th edn (Cambridge, 1852).

INDEX OF NAMES

INDEX OF SUBJECTS

94, 107, 114, 131, 167
Assent, Notional 22, 28, 34, 70,
71–3, 75, 76, 77, 78, 81, 87,
136, 140, 155, 164, 169
　Credence 71, 72
　Opinion 71, 72
　Presumption 71, 72
　Profession 71, 72
　Speculation 71, 73
Assent, Real 22, 70, 71, 73–7,
78, 85, 87, 88, 117, 136,
139, 143, 155, 164, 165
　Belief 76
Assertion 67, 68, 69, 70, 71, 80,
87, 98, 131
Association, Theories of 6, 7
Astronomy 110, 185
Authority 25, 69, 76, 83, 104,
125, 137
*Autobiographical Writings, John
Henry Newman:* x, xx, xxi,
16–18, 118, 177

Being 8, 20, 21, 22, 26, 27, 29,
31, 34, 42, 48, 52, 53, 54,
55, 57, 59, 60, 61, 62, 64,
71, 73, 74, 75, 76, 77, 78,
113, 117, 118, 122, 123,
129, 131, 133, 135, 136,
139, 150, 151, 152, 153,
154, 155, 156, 157, 166,
168, 171, 173, 181
　Analogy of 61
　Individual 21, 22, 52, 53, 55,
57, 59, 60, 61, 71, 77, 96,
117, 136, 154, 155, 157,
168
　Metaphysics of 21, 31, 42,
150, 171
　Participation of 23, 31, 42, 61,
157, 159

of Reason 60, 64
Belief *see* Assent, Real
Bibliography ix, 177–85
Birmingham Oratory Archives x,
18, 178

Calculus 13, 60, 108, 110, 112,
126, 142
Cartesian 35, 86
Catholic x, xiv, xvi xvii, xix, 11,
12, 16, 59, 177, 179, 180,
182
Causality xiii, 21, 25, 28–31, 39,
49, 102, 157, 159
Cause xii, xiii, 14, 21, 28–31, 39,
41, 49, 102, 141, 172
　Contingent 25, 31
　Efficient 31
　Final 30, 31, 128
　First 30, 31
　Necessary 30, 31, 102
　Physical 31, 102, 128, 141
　Secondary 31
*Certain Difficulties Felt by
Anglicans in Catholic
Teaching* x, 18, 146, 177
Certainty *see* Certitude
Certitude 27, 34, 62, 68, 81,
85–92, 99, 105, 106, 109,
121, 122, 124, 126, 131,
139, 141, 151, 156, 161, 168
　Certainty x, xviii, 6, 10, 33,
68, 79, 80, 81, 85, 86, 99,
101, 103, 104, 105, 121,
178
　Indefectibility of 88–90
　Token of 86
　Virtual 87
Chemistry 4
Commerce 94
Common Sense 2, 7, 10, 41, 109,

Printed in the United Kingdom
by Lightning Source UK Ltd.
118871UK00002B/67-198